VERY SHORT INTRODUCTIONS are for anyone wanting a stimulating and accessible way in to a new subject. They are written by experts, and have been published in more than 25 languages worldwide.

The series began in 1995, and now represents a wide variety of topics in history, philosophy, religion, science, and the humanities. Over the next few years it will grow to a library of around 250 volumes – a Very Short Introduction to everything from ancient Egypt and Indian philosophy to conceptual art and cosmology.

Very Short Introductions available now:

ANARCHISM   Colin Ward
ANCIENT EGYPT   Ian Shaw
ANCIENT PHILOSOPHY
  Julia Annas
ANCIENT WARFARE
  Harry Sidebottom
ANGLICANISM   Mark Chapman
THE ANGLO-SAXON AGE
  John Blair
ANIMAL RIGHTS   David DeGrazia
ARCHAEOLOGY   Paul Bahn
ARCHITECTURE
  Andrew Ballantyne
ARISTOTLE   Jonathan Barnes
ART HISTORY   Dana Arnold
ART THEORY   Cynthia Freeland
THE HISTORY OF
  ASTRONOMY   Michael Hoskin
ATHEISM   Julian Baggini
AUGUSTINE   Henry Chadwick
BARTHES   Jonathan Culler
THE BIBLE   John Riches
THE BRAIN   Michael O'Shea
BRITISH POLITICS
  Anthony Wright
BUDDHA   Michael Carrithers
BUDDHISM   Damien Keown
BUDDHIST ETHICS
  Damien Keown
CAPITALISM   James Fulcher
THE CELTS   Barry Cunliffe

CHOICE THEORY
  Michael Allingham
CHRISTIAN ART   Beth Williamson
CHRISTIANITY   Linda Woodhead
CLASSICS   Mary Beard and
  John Henderson
CLAUSEWITZ   Michael Howard
THE COLD WAR   Robert McMahon
CONSCIOUSNESS   Susan Blackmore
CONTEMPORARY ART
  Julian Stallabrass
CONTINENTAL PHILOSOPHY
  Simon Critchley
COSMOLOGY   Peter Coles
THE CRUSADES
  Christopher Tyerman
CRYPTOGRAPHY
  Fred Piper and Sean Murphy
DADA AND SURREALISM
  David Hopkins
DARWIN   Jonathan Howard
THE DEAD SEA SCROLLS
  Timothy Lim
DEMOCRACY   Bernard Crick
DESCARTES   Tom Sorell
DESIGN   John Heskett
DINOSAURS   David Norman
DREAMING   J. Allan Hobson
DRUGS   Leslie Iversen
THE EARTH   Martin Redfern
EGYPTIAN MYTH   Geraldine Pinch

For more information visit our web site

www.oup.co.uk/general/vsi/

EVERYTHING

A Very Short Introduction

OXFORD
UNIVERSITY PRESS

OXFORD
UNIVERSITY PRESS

Great Clarendon Street, Oxford OX2 6DP

Oxford University Press is a department of the University of Oxford.
It furthers the University's objective of excellence in research, scholarship,
and education by publishing worldwide in

Oxford New York

Auckland Cape Town Dar es Salaam Hong Kong Karachi
Kuala Lumpur Madrid Melbourne Mexico City Nairobi
New Delhi Shanghai Taipei Toronto

With offices in

Argentina Austria Brazil Chile Czech Republic France Greece
Guatemala Hungary Italy Japan Poland Portugal Singapore
South Korea Switzerland Thailand Turkey Ukraine Vietnam

Oxford is a registered trade mark of Oxford University Press
in the UK and in certain other countries

Published in the United States
by Oxford University Press Inc., New York

British Library Cataloguing in Publication Data

Data available

Library of Congress Cataloging in Publication Data

Data available

Typeset by RefineCatch Ltd, Bungay, Suffolk
Printing in China by Imago

ISBN 0-19-920819-0   978-0-19-920819-7

Contents

List of illustrations

The publisher and the author apologize for any errors or omissions in the above list. If contacted they will be pleased to rectify these at the earliest opportunity.

Very Short Introductions: A Very Short History

The *Very Short Introductions* series is phenomenally successful, enjoying widespread critical acclaim. Perfect for train journeys, holidays, and as a quick catch-up for busy people who want something intellectually stimulating, the carefully selected authors combine authoritative analysis, new ideas, and enthusiasm to provide much more than a straightforward introduction to each topic.

These vibrant and accessible books can change the way you think about the things that interest you, and are the perfect introduction to subjects you previously knew nothing about. From a lucid explanation of the essential issues in *Islam* to a lively insight into the complex theory of *Poststructuralism*, and a non-technical assessment of the very matter that makes up the universe in *Cosmology*, *Very Short Introductions* make often challenging topics highly readable and have proven to be extremely popular with general readers, as well as undergraduate students and their lecturers.

The series was originally launched in 1995 with the first title, *Classics: A Very Short Introduction*, and has quickly grown to become *the* general introduction series for the intelligent reader worldwide, being translated into over 20 languages. It will expand into a library of around 250 titles covering a wide range of key topics, from *The Brain* to *Ancient Egypt*, *Music* to *Buddhist Ethics*, in subject areas such as history, philosophy, science, religion, politics, and the arts.

2006 sees the publication of the 150th title in the series, *The Roman Empire*. This collection – *Everything, A Very Short Introduction* – has been put together to give you a taste of the series, with articles by seven of the authors on their subject area, as well as snapshots of each title.

Chapter 1
How on earth did we get here?

Introduction   Philip Ball

In 1638 two men met in a villa in Arcetri, near Florence. One was a precocious thirty-year-old Englishman, the other an ageing and grey-bearded Italian natural philosopher. Under house arrest by order of the Roman Church, Galileo was used to receiving visitors curious about his astronomical theory, and his young guest may have left little impression. But John Milton did not forget the meeting.

When twenty years later Milton began his most famous work, the epic poem *Paradise Lost*, the memory of Galileo must have haunted him. He had been appalled by the unjust treatment meted out to the sage of Pisa, and in his passionate defence of the freedom of speech, *Areopagitica* (1644), he had described how Galileo's imprisonment by the Inquisition 'for thinking in Astronomy otherwise than the Franciscan and Dominican licensers thought' had 'damped the glory of Italian wits'. Yet what is the universe of *Paradise Lost* but the conventional hierarchical cosmos of Ptolemy, endorsed by Christian theologians, with the heavens above and hell below a static earth?

Samuel Johnson criticized *Paradise Lost* for its 'harsh and barbarous' prose, but it is hard today not to feel more critical of Milton's decision to ignore Galileo's science. Perhaps he felt justified in taking poetic licence, retaining a stage design that fitted his narrative. But Galileo's universe, with the sun at its centre and the earth a mere planet in motion, probably left him deeply discomforted too. Certainly that seems to have been John Donne's feeling in 1611:

> And new Philosophy calls all in doubt,
> The Element of fire is quite put out;
> The Sun is lost, and th'earth, and no mans wit
> Can well direct him where to looke for it.

Today we find it intriguing and noteworthy when writers, poets, and artists look for inspiration and metaphor in science. In the 17th century that was a perfectly normal and deeply serious enterprise: John Donne, for all his misgivings, travelled to remote Linz in Austria to visit Johannes Kepler.

Clearly, those of a literary or artistic persuasion did not always like what they found in science; but that did not exempt them from the obligation to be appraised of the metaphysical implications of new discoveries. Milton's dilemma exemplifies the tensions between (to put it in stereotypical terms) the personal world-view of the artist and the objective perspective of the scientist; for Milton realized, even if he could not bring himself to articulate it, that things are not always as they seem, or as people believe them to be – or indeed, as we would like them to be.

In cosmological terms that lesson is still being learnt, while things have gone on getting ever stranger. Even Albert Einstein found himself misled by preconceptions when, in 1917, he fudged his equations describing a mathematical model of the universe to make it static and unchanging, as he though it should be. When, 12 years later, Edwin Hubble discovered that the universe is expanding, Einstein admitted his 'blunder' – if he'd not been blinkered by expectations, he'd have been able to predict Hubble's finding.

That discovery, meanwhile, revised Galileo (and his predecessor Nicolas Copernicus) once again. Astronomers had long since displaced the sun from the centre of the universe: it is merely the centre of our solar system, on the fringes of our galaxy, in an undistinguished corner of an immeasurably vast cosmos. But now this universe had a beginning. Play the Hubble expansion backwards and all converges to a point: the eye of the Big Bang, as maverick astronomer Fred Hoyle dismissively named this moment of creation.

For astronomy, the post-Copernican era had been a voyage into both revelation and ignorance. We know our place now; but the

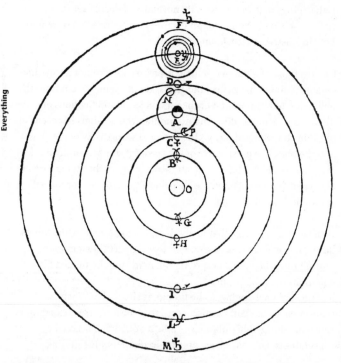

1. Galileo's presentation of the Copernican universe in his *Dialogue*. Unlike in Copernicus' representation, the earth is not alone in carrying a satellite.

cosmos is as mysterious as ever, arguably even more so. We know (or think we know) that most of the mass in the universe is invisible to us, and of unknown and exotic nature. Thanks to observations made over the past decade, we know (or think we know) that the universe is not just expanding but accelerating, seeming to imply that all of space is filled with some 'dark energy' that counteracts gravity and pushes everything apart. One interpretation is that Einstein was right after all to add a fudge factor (called the cosmological constant) to his equations – it was no blunder. We know, in other words, not to be too certain about anything.

Indeed, fundamental physics is more wide open a field than it has been for decades. At the scales of the very big and the very small our finest theories are not only glaringly incomplete but inconsistent. That is why Einstein himself now needs revising, although there is nothing like a consensus about how to do it. String theory and its rivals work beyond the horizons of what is readily testable, and so remain as yet closer to abstract mathematics than to science.

Even the understanding of our own planet has been altered almost beyond recognition in the past one hundred years. The ground on which we stand, the archetype of solidity, has become a constantly shifting mosaic thanks to the theory of continental drift introduced (to much derision, if not exactly Galilean persecution) by Alfred Wegener in the 1930s. The continental plates are merely a veneer, riding on a mantle of hot, extremely viscous rock that churns in great overturning rolls in the earth's bowels, rearranging the face of the planet over millions of years. In other words, not only our cosmic maps but even our world maps are but snapshots, destined one day for redundancy.

By the same token, we are forced to accept the contingency of our climate, our seas, and our atmosphere. The ice ages, first identified by Swiss geologist Louis Agassiz in the 1830s, forced scientists to take a dynamic view of the natural environment, culminating in the 'astronomical theory' of climate change due to Serbian mathematician Milutin Milankovitch in the 1920s. Periodic changes in the shape of the earth's orbit around the sun lead to 'Milankovitch cycles' which, as they phase in and out of step with one another, create a complex but predictable change in the temperatures of the earth's surface. Climate science has been one of the most revolutionary of the earth sciences over the past two decades, revealing natural processes that, riding on the back of the orbital variations, can transform the global climate in a matter of decades, melting the ice caps entirely or plunging the globe into cold storage.

But surely nothing would have unsettled Milton and his contemporaries as much as the discoveries of the past two centuries in the life sciences. Milton's Adam became first the descendant of an ape, as the Victorians crudely put it (that descent is still being painstakingly traced from a sparse yet constantly surprising fossil record), and then a 'machine created by our genes': an automaton at the mercy of segments of the DNA molecule. This seems to be the new frontier at which the debates between science, art, belief, and society will unfold. Arguably this frontier now has its milestone, comparable to Copernicus's *De revolutionibus* or Darwin's *Origin of Species*: the (more or less) complete sequence of the human genome, unveiled in 2001. (But let's not forget that this was a technological, not an intellectual, triumph.) Today questions about how much of our personality and our health are determined by our genetic inheritance, or how much of our personality and our health are determined by our genetic inheritance, or how a web of neurons becomes conscious of itself, seem to hold within them fundamental clues about what it is to be human. We would surely all appreciate a short introduction to that.

Cosmology   **Peter Coles**

What is it?

Cosmology is everything that exists. The entire system of things that is the Universe encompasses the very large and the very small – the astronomical scale of stars and galaxies and the microscopic world of elementary particles. The aim of cosmology is to place all known physical phenomena within a single coherent framework. This is an ambitious goal, and significant gaps in our knowledge still remain. Nevertheless, there has been such rapid progress that many cosmologists regard this as something of a 'Golden Age'. An emerging consensus about the form and distribution of matter and energy in the Universe suggests that a complete understanding of it all may be within reach. But if history tells us anything, it is that we should expect surprises!

> *'Buy and read this book even if you never thought you were interested in cosmology. It is a masterpiece of lucidity.'*

New Humanist

Particle Physics   **Frank Close**

The neutrino

Along with no electric charge, the neutrino has almost no mass and goes through almost everything. Oblivious to the normal electrical forces that act within bulk matter, neutrinos are hard to detect. It is figuratively the most nugatory of the particles.

The neutrino is the first 'fossil' relic of the Big Bang, and a messenger from the earliest processes in the universe. Neutrinos determine how fast the universe is expanding, and may determine its ultimate destiny. In stars like the Sun, they are essential in helping to cook the heavy elements that are necessary for life. The Sun is powered by the fusion of protons near its centre bumping into one another, joining and building up the nuclei of helium. In doing so some protons turn into neutrons by a form of beta radioactivity, and neutrinos are emitted as this happens. The effect is enormous: neutrinos are produced in the Sun at a rate of 2×10^{38} each second. That's two followed by 38 zeros; I cannot even imagine how to give an idea of how huge that number is – it's like the relative size of the whole universe to the size of a single atom. These neutrinos fly out into space and many hit Earth. About 400 billion neutrinos from the Sun pass through each one of us each second.

Neutrinos from the Sun fly through matter almost unchecked, so as many fly up through our beds at night as shine down on our heads by day. One of these neutrinos could fly through a light year of lead without hitting anything. This property of the neutrino is frequently mentioned in popular articles, and begs an obvious question: how do we detect them?

The History of Astronomy **Michael Hoskin**

Astronomy's long history

Historians of astronomy work mainly with the surviving documents from the past, and with artefacts such as instruments and observatory buildings. But can we discover something of the role the sky played in the 'cosmovision' of those who lived in Europe and the Middle East *before* the invention of writing? Could there even have been a prehistoric science of astronomy, perhaps one that enabled an elite to predict eclipses?

Stonehenge, for example, faces midsummer sunrise in one direction and midwinter sunset in the other. How can we be sure that an alignment that to us is of astronomical significance was chosen by Stonehenge's architects for this very reason? Did it have some quite different motivation, or even occur purely by chance? To take another example, a monument built around 3000 BC that faces east may have been oriented on the rising of the Pleiades, a bright cluster of stars in the constellation Taurus. It may have faced midway between midsummer and midwinter sunrise. Perhaps there was a sacred mountain in that direction. Or the orientation may have been chosen simply to take advantage of the slope of the ground. How can we decide which of these, if any, was in the minds of the builders?

The Earth   **Martin Redfern**

How can you put a big round planet in a small flat book?

It is not an easy fit, but there could be two broadly different ways of attempting it. One is the bottom-up approach of geology: essentially, looking at the rocks. For centuries, geologists have scurried around on the surface of our planet with their little hammers, examining the different rock types and the mineral grains which make them up. With eye and microscope, electron probe and mass spectrometer, they have reduced the planet to its component parts. Then they have mapped out how the different rock types relate to one another and, through theory, observation, and experiment, they have worked out how they might have got there. It has been a huge undertaking and one that has brought deep insights. Collectively, the efforts of all those geologists have built a giant edifice on which future earth scientists can stand. But this introduction is not a guide to rocks and minerals and geological map-making. It is a portrait of a planet.

2. Planet earth, as seen from space

The new view on our old planet is the top-down approach of what has come to be known as earth systems science. It looks at the earth as a whole, and not just frozen in time in the moment we call now. Taken over the deep time of geology we begin to see our planet as a dynamic system, a series of processes and cycles. We can begin to understand what makes it tick.

The Elements   **Philip Ball**

So how many elements are there? I do not know, and neither does anyone else. Oh, they can tell you how many *natural* elements there are – how many we can expect to find at large in the universe. *That* series stops around uranium, element number 92. But as to how many elements are possible – well, name a number. We have no idea what the limit might be.

Chemists and physicists have collaborated since the middle of the twentieth century to make new elements: substances never before seen on Earth. They are expanding the Periodic Table, step by painful step, into uncharted realms where it becomes increasingly hard to predict which elements might form and how they might behave. This is the field of nuclear chemistry. Instead of shuffling elements into new combinations – molecules and compounds – as most chemists do, nuclear chemists are coercing subatomic particles (protons and neutrons) to combine in new liaisons within atomic nuclei.

> '*A delight of a book. . . . Elegantly written . . . it's far-reaching, entertaining and salted with anecdote. . . . It could become a classic. Hold on to your first edition.*'
>
> Roy Herbert, *New Scientist*

Molecules   Philip Ball

Material genes

One way of making artificial silk polymer is to import silk-making genes into bacteria using biotechnological techniques. Just like any other protein, silk is genetically encoded in DNA: the sequence of its amino acids along the chains is determined by a corresponding sequence of nucleotide units in a gene in the spider's chromosomes. In other words, the spider possesses a molecular blueprint for making the polymer. (But notice how, because of the complexities of the spinning process, this blueprint alone is not enough to make good silk threads!)

The ability of living organisms to define the molecular composition of a polymer with complete accuracy is an enviable one. Modern synthetic techniques allow chemists a great deal of control over the composition of a chain – for example, they can make hybrid polymers by grafting side chains of one chemical type into a main chain of another, or by alternating between blocks of one type of unit and blocks of another along a single chain. But making a polymer perhaps thousands of units long in which many different units recur in a sequence of arbitrary complexity – and yet with every molecular chain in the material being identical – is something far beyond our current synthetic capabilities. In a linguistic analogy, our state-of-the-art polymers read something like this: aaaaaaabbbbbbbaaaaaaabbbbbbbaa. . . Nature's polymers, meanwhile, are more like this entire sentence, and pregnant with meaning.

Galileo   Stillman Drake

Galileo's significance for the formation of modern science lies partly in his discoveries and opinions in physics and astronomy, but much more in his refusal to allow science to be guided any longer by philosophy. By stages, his rejection of the long-established authority of philosophers induced them to appeal to the Bible for support, and there ensued a battle for freedom of scientific enquiry which profoundly affected the development of modern society, leading to a final parting of the ways between science and philosophy. In a startling reinterpretation of the evidence, Stillman Drake advances the hypothesis that Galileo's trial and condemnation by the Inquisition in 1633 was caused not by his defiance of the Church, but by the hostility of contemporary philosophers.

Quantum Theory   **John Polkinghorne**

It is no exaggeration to regard the discovery (in the mid-1920s) of quantum theory as being one of the most outstanding intellectual achievements of the 20th century and as constituting a real revolution in our understanding of the physical world since the days of Isaac Newton. What had been considered to be the arena of clear and determinate process was found to be, at its subatomic roots, cloudy and fitful in its behaviour. Compared with this revolutionary change, the great discoveries of special and general relativity seem not much more than interesting variations on classical themes. Indeed, Albert Einstein, who had been the progenitor of relativity theory, found modern quantum mechanics so little to his metaphysical taste that he remained implacably opposed to it right to the end of his life.

If the study of quantum physics teaches one anything, it is that the world is full of surprises. No one would have supposed beforehand that there could be entities that sometimes behaved as if they were waves and sometimes behaved as if they were particles. This realization was forced upon the physics community by the intransigent necessity of actual empirical experience. As Bohr once said, the world is not only stranger than we thought; it is stranger than we could think. Even logic has to be modified when it is applied to the quantum world.

Darwin   **Jonathan Howard**

Focusing on Darwin's major insights and arguments, Jonathan Howard reasserts the importance of Darwin's work for the development of modern science and culture.

Darwin's contribution to biology

The whole point of understanding the modern theory of evolution is to understand that human life and human society are to a certain extent biological issues, painfully difficult to deal with in these terms, but still biology. For this reason, this introduction keeps strictly to the core of the matter, which is Darwin's contribution to biology. Darwinian philosophy or Darwinian society are *post-hoc* constructs that had no place in Darwin's thought. He was unable to see how evolution in biology could have any but the feeblest analogical resemblance to the evolution of society. The complete separation between social and political philosophy and Darwin's Darwinism is the main justification, if any is needed, for dealing only with the latter. The biology is where the issues are finally grounded, and it is probably the biology that is least generally known.

Evolution   **Brian and Deborah Charlesworth**

We are all one with creeping things;
And apes and men
Blood-brethren.

From *Drinking Song*, Thomas Hardy

What can we learn from evolution?

Science tells us that human beings are the product of impersonal forces, and that the habitable world forms a minute part of a universe of immense size and duration. Whatever the religious or philosophical beliefs of individual scientists, the whole programme of scientific research is founded on the assumption that the universe can be understood on such a basis.

Few would dispute that this programme has been spectacularly successful, particularly in the 20th century, which saw such terrible events in human affairs. The influence of science may have indirectly contributed to these events, partly through the social changes triggered by the rise of industrial mass societies, and partly through the undermining of traditional belief systems.

The study of evolution has revealed our intimate connections with the other species that inhabit the earth. The purpose of this book is to introduce the reader to some of the most important basic findings, concepts, and procedures of evolutionary biology, as it has developed since the first publications of Darwin and Wallace on the subject, over 140 years ago. Evolution provides a set of unifying principles for the whole of biology; it also illuminates the relation of human beings to the universe and to each other.

Mathematics   **Timothy Gowers**

This is an attempt to convey the spirit of advanced mathematics while making very few demands on the reader's prior knowledge and technical competence. This is notoriously hard to do in a subject that is full of complicated arguments and long calculations, often couched in jargon that appears to be utterly impenetrable.

The book does not try to explain any jargon or present difficult arguments and calculations in detail: even if this were desirable it would be impossible to do satisfactorily in a short introduction.

Instead, it has the more modest aim of elucidating a few of the more challenging *concepts* of mathematics, concepts such as infinity, the square roots of negative numbers, curved space, and geometry in four or more dimensions.

The way to understand these counterintuitive ideas is to begin with much simpler ones. An important message of the book is that even a concept as basic as that of a natural number (that is, one of the numbers 1,2,3,4,5, . . . etc.) involves significant subtleties. Implicit in our understanding of the natural numbers is an acceptance of various arithmetical rules, which, after many years of schooling, we come to use unquestioningly, to the point where we hardly notice that we are doing so. Why, for example, is it easy to see that 50 times 40 = 2000? One possible justification is to say that 50 times 40 = (5 times 10) times (4 times 10) = (5 times 4) times (10 times 10) = 20 times 100 = 2000. This argument may be convincing, but in the course of it we appeal to various arithmetical principles, such as that (ab) times (cd) must equal (ac) times (bd) for any four numbers a, b, c, and d.

Simple rules such as these are important for two reasons: they are what we use to think about numbers in a general context, and they help us define new sorts of numbers.

> '. . . includes so much useful information and ideas it is quite incredible.'
>
> The Times

Fossils   **Keith Thomson**

In the beginning

The biggest gaps in the fossil record are right at the beginning. No rocks survive in the earth's crust that are older than about 3.9 byr, all earlier rocks having been recycled by earth processes. The period between the earth forming some 4.5 byr ago and the beginning of the Cambrian, 545 myr ago, is defined as the Precambrian Aeon, divided into three Eras (first the Hadean; then the Archaean, beginning 4 byr ago; and most recently, 2.5 byr ago, the Proterozoic, meaning 'first life').

A small amount of evidence, mostly still controversial, records the presence of bacteria and perhaps other microbial life in Archaean rocks from Australia and South Africa dated at 3.5 byr ago. The principal kinds of bacteria were cyanobacteria: the name refers to the blue-green colour, not the production of cyanide. Cyanobacteria are still abundant on earth today. There is, however, a gap of at least a billion years between the formation of the earth and these first signs of living organisms. At some point in that interval, life arose on earth in the form of relatively simple self-replicating molecules and proceeded to the formation of something like modern viruses and bacteria.

Dinosaurs   **David Norman**

David Norman reveals how scientists combine anatomy, genetics, forensics, and even engineering design to build a picture of what dinosaurs looked like, what they ate, and how they moved and interacted with each other. Exploring how animal life evolved on Earth, he highlights the place of dinosaurs in evolutionary history.

Dinosaurs and birds

First and foremost, it is now clear that feathers do not, after all, make a bird. Various sorts of skin coverings appear to have been present on a wide range of theropod dinosaurs, ranging from a shaggy, filamentous type of covering, through downy, feather-like body coverings, to fully formed contour and flight feathers. The discoveries at Liaoning force us to wonder just how widespread such body coverings might have been, not only among theropods, but, perhaps, even in other dinosaur groups as well. Given the known distribution of body coverings, it is not unreasonable to ponder the probability of giants such as *Tyrannosaurus rex* (which was a theropod related to *Sinosauropteryx*) having some sort of epidermal covering – even if only as juveniles. Such tantalizing questions cannot be answered at present, and require the discovery of new geological deposits similar in quality of fossil preservation to those at Liaoning.

Human Evolution   **Bernard Wood**

The 'long' version of human evolution would be a journey that starts approximately three billion years ago at the base of the Tree of Life (TOL) with the simplest form of life. We would then pass up the base of the trunk and into the relatively small part of the tree that contains all animals, and on into the branch that contains all the animals with backbones. Around 400 million years ago we would enter the branch that contains vertebrates that have four limbs, then around 250 million years ago into the branch that contains the mammals, and then into a thin branch that contains one of the subgroups of mammals called the primates. At the base of this primate branch we are still at least 50–60 milion years away from the present day.

The next part of this 'long' version of the human evolutionary journey takes us successively into the monkey and ape, the ape and then into the great ape branches of the Tree of Life. Sometime between 15 and 12 million years ago we move into the small branch that gave rise to contemporary modern humans and to the living African apes. Between 11 and 9 million years ago the branch for the gorillas split off to leave just a single slender branch consisting of the ancestors of both extant (i.e. living) chimpanzees and modern humans. Around 8 to 5 million years ago this very small branch split into two twigs. One of the twigs ends on the surface of the TOL with the living chimpanzees, the other leads to modern humans. Palaeoanthropology is the science that tries to reconstruct the evolutionary history of this small, exclusively human, twig.

Philosophy of Science   **Samir Okasha**

Samir Okasha investigates the nature of scientific reasoning, scientific explanation, revolutions in science, and theories such as realism and anti-realism.

Why is this important?

Scientific ideas change fast. Pick virtually any scientific discipline, and you can be sure that the prevalent theories in that discipline will be very different from those of 50 years ago, and extremely different from those of 100 years ago. A number of interesting philosophical questions centre on the issue of scientific change. Is there a discernible pattern to the way scientific ideas change over time? When scientists abandon their existing theory in favour of a new one, how should we explain this? Are later scientific theories objectively better than earlier ones? Or does the concept of objectivity make sense at all?

> *'This book gives an excellent sense of what keeps philosophers of science awake at night. The issues and the arguments are presented with stunning clarity.'*
>
> Peter Lipton, University of Cambridge

The End of the World   **Bill McGuire**

Global warming is with us now and we know that within several thousand years the ice is due to return, but other threats to our comfortable existence are less predictable. *The End of the World* also takes a close look at the latest research findings to elucidate the threats posed by the enormous geological forces building beneath our planet's surface. A collapsing volcano in the Canary Islands threatens to crash into the North Atlantic, generating giant sea waves capable of swamping the great cities of the eastern United States. Somewhere in Southeast Asia or around the Pacific Rim, a giant volcanic blast capable of blacking out the sun for years and leading to global freezing and starvation is well overdue. More imminently, a huge quake is forecast to strike Tokyo in the next few

Everything

3. A possible end to the world? An atomic explosion

decades, causing destruction totalling 7 trillion US$ and triggering global economic meltdown.

So far we have been lucky, but good fortune cannot last forever. Short of a so-called 'extinction-level event', such as the huge comet impact that ended the dinosaurs' long reign, it is unlikely that any other foreseeable natural event will be capable of wiping out all 6 billion of us. It is equally unlikely, however, that our race and our modern society will continue to thrive without being knocked back, perhaps more than once, by a global natural catastrophe so large that there will be nowhere to run to and nowhere to hide.

Forthcoming
Chaos, Leonard Smith
Newton, Robert Iliffe

Chapter 2

There's more to us than meets the eye

Introduction   **Simon Blackburn**

There are theorems in logic that as you ascend to do the theory of a theory, you need more powerful methods and get less solid results than if you stay down below. The same kind of result applies to writing a very short introduction to Very Short Introductions. Yet anyone browsing these amazing little books will recognize that philosophy lends itself ideally to very short introductions. For apart from dry and dedicated specialists, few people remember anything more of even favourite philosophers than some very short sound bites.

Philosophy may or may not be as Milton described it: 'a perpetual feast of nectar'd sweets, where no crude surfeit reigns'. It is arguably unique among subjects in that a lot of its practitioners spend a lot of their time wondering what it is. Is it an art or a science? Does it discover things in the sense of uncovering truths that were always waiting to be revealed? Or does it discover things in the sense in which someone might discover a new way to entertain teenagers, or play King Lear? Should it aspire to the condition of mathematics, or the condition of music: truth, entertainment, or something else again?

Traditionally, philosophy means reflection on some concepts that structure a lot of our thought – big concepts, such as truth, reason, objectivity, knowledge, goodness, God, the soul, freedom, virtue, and meaning. And it means studying the writers whose reflections on those big concepts have been important, or still speak to us now. But after that, things become less clear. Why do some concepts, but not others, get on to the list? And what distinguishes the philosopher from the mere preacher, on the one hand, and from the other people licensed to reflect upon the human condition, such as writers of fiction, poets, and dramatists, on the other hand? Admittedly, the dividing lines are sometimes thin, since some philosophers, such as Plato or Nietzsche, are rather like poets, and others, such as Marx or Engels or Augustine, are frequently not so far from being preachers. Rousseau wrote novels, and Hume wrote excellent dialogue. Perhaps there is no way of drawing a sharp boundary. If someone reflects about how things hang together, in the most general sense of the term, perhaps that is enough to qualify them as a philosopher.

But then what does reflection mean here? A philosopher is neither a laboratory scientist, nor a social scientist armed with a clipboard or a set of statistics. Some philosophers, especially in the contemporary world, like to think of themselves as closely allied to the natural sciences, and some, such as Descartes, have been distinguished natural scientists themselves. But the lack of experimental practice makes the alliance with natural science a bit suspect, to say the least. It is as if the philosopher sets himself up as a maker of maps who needs to make no observations and take no measurements. For Kant, this was the central puzzle in the whole theory of knowledge. The possibility that the mind, by simple self-conscious reflection, should obtain knowledge about its own nature and the nature of its world was sufficiently strange to require the *Critique of Pure Reason* to lay it to rest.

Unfortunately, not even Kant's 800 pages could do that. A definitive story of the scope and limits of human reflection would tell us, for instance, whether there is progress in philosophy, and, if not, why we are condemned to trudge permanently around the same maze. For Hegel there is indeed progress, and the whole of human history is the progress of a kind of self-consciousness. Although as Peter

Singer engagingly points out in his contribution on Hegel, the German word *Selbstbewusstsein* has more the flavour of self-assertion than the English word self-consciousness, with its hint of introspection or even embarrassment, and it is perhaps easier to see history as a progress of human beings throwing their weight about rather than a progress of anything more contemplative.

In his book in this series, *Philosophy: A Very Short Introduction*, Edward Craig reminds us how natural it is to human beings to find themselves reflecting on their world, and the success or failure of their pursuits, and the hidden forces to which they might appeal to do better. Philosophies of life try to systematize these answers, most obviously in the texts that form the basis of religious systems. Religion is the first expression of the philosophical impulse. Science is the second, and it is of course a first-rate philosophical question whether it supersedes and displaces the first, or whether it can live alongside it. We will write the history of self-consciousness very differently according to how we answer this question.

If philosophy were like religion, then it might decay, and if it were like mathematics, only done with words, it might progress. Perhaps the best answer strips Hegel of his confidence, and contents itself with allowing that in so far as humanity progresses, so will philosophy progress with it, and in so far as humanity merely changes, so will philosophy merely change with it. My own *Ethics: A Very Short Introduction* supposes that subjectivism and relativism, as well as misapplications of evolutionary and biological theory, get in the way of ethical thinking, now more than ever. Here, we may actually have gone backwards.

Where does philosophy stand now? And where is it going? If we suppose, with Hegel, Marx, or Foucault, that philosophical reflection is always motivated by general cultural forces and anxieties, then it will be a question of what bothers us now, and will bother us in the future. It is difficult enough to answer the first. Indeed, it is impossible if we add the doctrine that those anxieties are standardly unconscious, so that at some deep level the concerns and the presuppositions of any particular time only become visible at another time, as self-consciousness distances itself from them. To take an example almost at random, as Julia Annas describes in her *Ancient Philosophy: A Very Short Introduction*, we can see the Victorians as anxious about government, and hence anxious to portray Plato as a kind of godfather of the civil service. But they were not themselves aware that this is what they were doing, or they could not have done it. Once it is self-conscious, the ideology becomes embarrassed.

In such a picture, the philosopher merely follows the parade. As Hegel put it, the owl of Minerva only takes wing with the coming of the night. But this seems wrong as well, for, after all, the literature of a time not only reflects that time, but helps mould the self-awareness and identity of those who follow and read it. We have only to think of Marx, or of the struggles of feminist writers to articulate an ideology, and their political successes when they did so. To paraphrase Nietzsche, ideas are explosions waiting to happen. But as for where philosophy is going, if this picture is right, we cannot predict that any more than we can predict the future. As is often said, if we could predict inventions, we would invent them. To have predicted a great philosopher would have been to have thought what he did before him, and then he wouldn't have been a great philosopher.

Philosophy and the philosophers described in this series give us a world literature. We don't know where literature is going. What we do know is how exciting it is to see where it has been. It is remarkable to have a resource giving us so much awareness of that, and one asking for such little effort from the reader.

Philosophy   **Edward Craig**

Philosophy is not an activity from another planet: learning about it is just a matter of broadening and deepening what most of us do already. In this lively and engaging book, Edward Craig shows that philosophy is no mere intellectual pastime; thinkers such as Plato, Descartes, Hegel, Darwin, Mill, and de Beauvoir, and Buddhist writers, were responding to real needs and events – much of their work shapes our lives today, and many of their concerns are still ours.

Anyone reading this book is to some extent a philosopher already. Nearly all of us are, because we have some kinds of values by which we live our lives (or like to think we do, or feel uncomfortable when we don't). And most of us favour some very general picture of what the world is like. Perhaps we think there's a god who made it all, including us; or, on the contrary, we think it's all a matter of chance and natural selection. Perhaps we believe that people have immortal, non-material parts called souls or spirits; or, quite the opposite, that we are just complicated arrangements of matter that gradually fall to bits after we die. So most of us, even those who don't *think about it* at all, have something like answers to the two basic philosophical questions, namely: what should we do? and, what is there?

> 'A vigorous and engaging introduction that speaks to the philosopher in everyone. Craig helps the reader grapple with some key texts and problems are carefully chosen to show how philosophical inquiry is something we should all care about.'

> John Cottingham, University of Reading

4. Cartoon from *Punch*

Political Philosophy   **David Miller**

This book introduces readers to the concepts of political philosophy. David Miller starts by explaining why the subject is important and how it tackles basic ethical questions such as 'how should we live together in society?' The book looks at political authority, the reasons why we need politics at all, the limitations of politics, and whether there are areas of life that shouldn't be governed by politics. It explores the connections between political authority and justice, a constant theme in political philosophy, and the ways in which social justice can be used to regulate rather than destroy a market economy. David Miller discusses why nations are the natural units of government and whether the rise of multiculturalism and transnational cooperation will change this: will we ever see the formation of a world government?

Ancient Philosophy   Julia Annas

The pursuit of a happy life

Happiness in ancient ethical thought is not a matter of feeling good or being pleased; it is not a feeling or emotion at all. It is your life as a whole which is said to be happy or not, and so discussions of happiness are discussions of the happy life. It is our bad luck that for us what is happy are not just lives, but also moments and fleeting experiences; modern discussions of happiness tend to get confused very rapidly because such different things are being considered. In ancient ethics, happiness enters by a very different route from the 'feel-good' one.

'Incisive, elegant, and full of the excitement of doing philosophy, [this book] boldly steps outside the conventional chronological ways of organizing material about the Greeks and Romans to get right to the heart of the human problems that exercised them ... I can't think of a better way to begin.'

Martha Nussbaum, University of Chicago

Presocratic Philosophy   Catherine Osborne

We call them Presocratic philosophers. 'Philosophers' because they seek after wisdom, or because we can detect some resemblance to the project we think of as philosophy, or both; 'Presocratic' because they precede Socrates in one or both of two senses. First, they were older than Socrates. Many were born well before 469 BC and all but a few had passed their prime before the end of the 5th century. But second, and more importantly, they are considered to have preceded Socrates in philosophical terms. Often, when thinking about Socrates (or about Plato's depiction of Socrates), we need to remember that he is reacting to the Presocratics, but the reverse is never true.

But interest in these early thinkers is not confined to their influence on the major figures of later philosophy; they are fascinating also for their own gestures towards the great questions of all time. They did not call themselves 'philosophers', or not in our sense of that word, nor did they have a conception of 'philosophy' as a definite range of enquiries. They set out in search of wisdom, what they called 'sophia'. Looking back at their searches we can say, with hindsight, that some of their investigations were taking them in directions that would swiftly become central to philosophy – philosophy as it emerged in Classical Greece, and as it is still practised in universities today.

Continental Philosophy   **Simon Critchley**

The author tells a story that begins with the publication of Kant's critical philosophy in the 1780s and includes discussions of major philosophers like Nietzsche, Heidegger, Foucault, and Kristeva. At the core of the book is a plea to place philosophy at the centre of cultural life, and thereby reawaken its primary definition of the love of wisdom that makes life worth living.

Principal strands of continental philosophy

1) German idealism and romanticism, and their aftermath (Fichte, Schelling, Hegel, Schlegel and Novalis, Schleiermacher, Schopenhauer)

2) The critique of metaphysics and the 'masters of suspicion' (Feuerbach, Marx, Nietzsche, Freud, Bergson)

3) Germanophone phenomenology and existential philosophy (Husserl, Max Scheler, Karl Jaspers, Heidegger)

4) French phenomenology, Hegelianism and anti-Hegelianism (Kojève, Sartre, Merleau-Ponty, Levinas, Bataille, de Beauvoir)

5) Hermeneutics (Dilthey, Gadamer, Ricoeur)

6) Western Marxism and the Frankfurt School (Lukács, Benjamin, Horkheimer, Adorno, Marcuse, Habermas)

7) French structuralism (Lévi-Strauss, Lacan, Althusser), post-structuralism (Foucault, Derrida, Deleuze), post-modernism (Lyotard, Baudrillard), and feminism (Irigaray, Kristeva)

Foucault   **Gary Gutting**

From aesthetics to the penal system, from madness and civilization to Nietsche and the avant-garde, the writings of Michel Foucault (1926–1984) had a powerful impact on modern thought in the late twentieth century. However, as wide-ranging and influential as his works are, they also have the reputation of being difficult and impenetrable.

Gary Gutting provides a compelling introduction to Foucault's work in the fields of literature, politics, history, and philosophy, and explores some of the key themes that fascinated the philosopher in his quest to more deeply understand identity, knowledge, and power in modern society.

'a first-rate introduction to the work of this difficult thinker which navigates the complexity of his thought with the confidence and clarity of one who has studied Foucault for years'

Todd May, Clemson University, South Carolina

Indian Philosophy   **Sue Hamilton**

From the earliest beginnings, philosophical debate in India developed, flourished, and proliferated into a variety of schools of thought. In highlighting its key features, the author draws the reader into the world of 'classical' Indian philosophy, illustrating the different ways in which the great Indian thinkers interpreted and sought to understand the nature of reality.

Understanding Indian philosophy

Westerners approaching the Indian tradition for the first time, whether their interest be primarily in religion or in philosophy, are faced with two equal and opposing problems. One is to find something graspable amid the apparently bewildering multiplicity; the other is not enforcing such a straitjacket on to the material as to overlook significant aspects of the diversity. The classic example of the latter is 'Hinduism': because of the existence of the name Hinduism, Westerners expect to find a monolithic tradition comparable to other 'isms'. They remain baffled by what they find until they discover that Hinduism is a label that was attached in the 19th century to a highly complex and multiple collection of systems of thought by other Westerners who did not appreciate that complexity.

> 'a wonderful job in capturing the profound wisdom embedded in Indian thought . . . compelling and extremely rewarding'
>
> Shlomo Biderman, University of Tel Aviv

> ' . . . the perfect gift for anyone who wishes to sort out their karma and nirvana'
>
> The Independent

Habermas   James Gordon Finlayson

Jürgen Habermas is one of the most influential philosophers alive today. His writings interweave social, moral, political, and legal theory to examine subjects ranging from Marxism to the European Union, and the role of communication and discourse in the modern world.

James Gordon Finlayson shows in clear, accessible language how Habermas' theory as a whole answers important questions about the nature of modern society, and how it can shape our views on contemporary issues and events.

The unfinished project of modernity

In 1980 Habermas caused a stir with his speech 'Modernity – an Unfinished Project' on the occasion of his receipt of the Adorno Prize. The speech was provocative because Habermas characteristically swam against the then strong intellectual tide of a post-modern movement anxious to bid farewell to modernity and the whole accompanying enlightenment project. Habermas's title implicitly makes two points. First, modernity is a *project* rather than an historical period; and second, this project is not yet (but can and should be) completed.

Animal Rights   David DeGrazia

Do animals have moral rights? If so, what does this mean? What sorts of mental lives do animals have, and how should we understand their welfare? After putting forward possible answers to these questions, David DeGrazia explores the implications for how we treat animals in connection with our diet, zoos, and research.

Do animals have souls?

One common contention is that animals lack awareness or consciousness because they lack *immortal souls*, conceived as immaterial substances. But this is an extremely weak argument. It ignores all empirical evidence for animal awareness while resting on an assumption for which there is no basis: that human beings but no other animals possess immortal souls. One wonders when exactly in hominid evolution our ancestors began to have souls!

Ethics   Simon Blackburn

This section looks at ideas that destabilize us when we think about standards of choice and conduct. In various ways they seem to suggest that ethics is somehow impossible. They are important because they themselves can seep into the moral environment. When they do, they can change what we expect from each other and ourselves, usually for the worse. Under their influence, when we look at the big words – justice, equality, freedom, rights – we see only bids for power and clashes of power, or we see only hypocrisy, or we see only our own opinions, unworthy to be foisted onto others.

Cynicism and self-consciousness paralyse us. In what follows we consider seven such threats:

1. The death of God
2. Relativism
3. Egoism
4. Evolutionary Theory
5. Determinism and futility
6. Unreasonable demands
7. False consciousness

> '*Simon Blackburn's short book takes the big moral questions head on and does so brilliantly . . . a witty, vivid writer with an enviable popular touch . . . this is a wonderfully enlightening book.*'
>
> Ben Rogers, *Sunday Telegraph*

Medical Ethics   **Tony Hope**

Ethical issues in medicine are rarely out of the media, and are of particular relevance to the general public and the medical practitioner alike. In this *Very Short Introduction*, Tony Hope deals with a range of thorny moral questions, some of which are age-old, like euthanasia and the morality of killing, and others of which have arisen with recent advances in medical technology.

Tony Hope also explores political questions, discussing how health-care resources an be fairly allocated, and addressing controversial problems such as: Should treatment for mental illness be imposed on patients without their consent? Should post-menopausal women have access to assisted reproduction technologies? And who should have the right to access information from genetic testing?

There's more to us than meets the eye

Choice Theory   Michael Allingham

We make choices all the time. We also constantly judge the decisions that other people make as rational or irrational. But what kinds of criteria are we applying when we say that a choice is rational, and what guides our own choices, especially in cases where we do not have complete information about the possible outcomes? This book explores what it means to be rational in all these contexts and shows that life is about making choices.

Choose rationally

> Choose life. Choose a job . . . Choose a big television . . . Choose good health, low cholesterol and dental insurance. Choose fixed-interest mortgage repayments . . . Choose your friends. Choose your future . . . Choose life.

All choices, just as Renton's opening voiceover (above) from the film *Trainspotting*, arise from both the heart and the head. But is he choosing rationally? The heart provides the passion and the head the reasons. Choices based on the most minute reasoning but lacking any desire are vacuous, while desire without reason is impotent: it is only fit for the enraged child

32

who wants both to go home and not to go home. Aristotle, the founder of choice theory, and indeed of logic itself, identifies the connection:

> 'The origin of . . . choice is desire and reasoning with a view to the end – this is why choice cannot exist without . . . reason.'

Logic   **Graham Priest**

Problem Solutions

You hire a car. If you do not take out insurance, and you have an accident, it will cost you $1,500. If you take out insurance, and have an accident, it will cost you $300. The insurance costs $90, and you estimate that the probability of an accident is 0.05. Assuming that the only considerations are financial ones, should you take out the insurance.

Tabulate the information as follows:

	Have an accident	Don't have an accident
Take out insurance (t)	0.05\–390	0.95\–90
Don't take out insurance ($\neg t$)	0.05\–1,500	0.95\–0

Calculating expectations, we get:

$E(t) = 0.05 \times (-390) + 0.95 \times (-90) = -105$
$E(\neg t) = 0.05 \times (-1,500) + 0.95 \times 0 = -75$

Since $E(\neg t) > E(t)$, you should not take out insurance.

> '. . . *a splendid feat of warming up logic for the general palate.*'
> The Guardian

Free Will   **Thomas Pink**

Every day we seem to make and act upon all kinds of free choices –

some trivial, and others so consequential that they may change the course of our life. But are these choices really free? Or are we compelled to act the way we do by factors beyond our control? Is the feeling that we could have made different decisions just an illusion? And if our choices are not free, is it legitimate to hold people morally responsible for their actions?

This *Very Short Introduction* looks at a range of issues surrounding this fundamental philosophical question. Exploring free will through the ideas of the Greek and medieval philosophers up to present-day thinkers, Thomas Pink provides an original and incisive introduction to this perennially fascinating subject, and a new defence of the reality of human free will.

The unfreedom of animals

So far we have been looking at the relation between freedom and determinism. But there is another important aspect to freedom that has not yet been discussed – the relation between freedom and reason. To see how important reason might be, we need to consider some beings who certainly perform actions, but who do so without having the control over how they act that we humans possess over our actions. We need to consider the animals.

I am not claiming that all non-human animals lack freedom. For example, it is a matter of dispute exactly how intelligent chimpanzees and dolphins really are – and perhaps they will turn out to be free agents too. I suspect, in fact, that chimpanzees and dolphins are not intelligent enough in the particular ways needed for freedom, but this is not the place to argue the matter. We do not yet know enough about precisely how capable these higher animals really are. There are however other, much less sophisticated animals whose capacities fall very far short of our own, and who do clearly lack freedom of action as a result.

Philosophy of Law   Raymond Wacks

Law as interpretation

The foundations of legal philosophy were shaken in the 1970s by the ideas of the American jurist, Ronald Dworkin (1931–), who in 1969 succeeded H. L. A. Hart as Professor of Jurisprudence at Oxford. Among the numerous elements of Dworkin's philosophy is the contention that the law contains a solution to almost every problem. This is at variance with the traditional – positivist – perception that when a judge is faced with a difficult case to which no statute or previous decision applies, he exercises a discretion, and decides the case on the basis of what seems to him to be the correct answer. Dworkin contests this position, and shows how a judge does not make law, but rather *interprets* what is already part of the legal material. Through his interpretation of these materials, he gives voice to the values to which the legal system is committed.

To understand Dworkin's key proposition that is a 'gapless' system, consider the following two situations:

An impatient beneficiary under a will murders the testator. Should he be permitted to inherit?

A chess grandmaster distracts his opponent by continually smiling at him. The opponent objects. Is smiling in breach of the rules of chess?

These are both 'hard cases' for in neither case is there a determinable rule to resolve it. This gives legal positivists a headache, for positivism generally claims that law consists of rules determined by social facts. Where, as in these examples, rules run out, the problem can be resolved only by the exercise of a subjective, and hence, potentially arbitrary, discretion: a nightmare.

Words of wisdom from VSI

Aristotle   **Jonathan Barnes**

Politicians have no leisure because they are always aiming at something beyond political life itself, power and glory, or happiness.

Plato   **Julia Annas**

Is that which is holy loved by the gods because it is holy, or is it holy because it is loved by the gods?

Socrates   **C. C. W. Taylor**

The unexamined life is not worth living.

Augustine   **Henry Chadwick**

Take up and read, take up and read.

Hobbes   **Richard Tuck**

Laughter is nothing else but sudden glory arising from some sudden conception of some eminency in ourselves, by comparison with the infirmity of others, or with our own formerly.

Descartes   **Tom Sorell**

Common sense is the best distributed commodity in the world, for every man is convinced that he is well supplied with it.

Spinoza   **Roger Scruton**

So far as in me lies, I value, above all other things out of my control, the joining hands of friendship with men who are lovers of truth.

Locke   **John Dunn**

New opinions are always suspected, and usually opposed, without any other reason but because they are not already common.

Hume   A. J. Ayer

The heart of man is made to reconcile the most glaring of contradictions.

Rousseau   **Robert Wokler**

Everything is good when it springs from the hands of our Creator; everything degenerates when shaped by the hands of man.

Kant   **Roger Scruton**

Many people imagine that the years of their youth are the pleasantest and best of their lives; but it is not really so. They are the most troublesome; for we are then under strict discipline, can seldom choose our friends, and still more seldom have our freedom.

Hegel   **Peter Singer**

What experience and history can tell us is this – that nations and governments have never learned anything from history, or acted upon any lessons they might have drawn from it.

Clausewitz   **Michael Howard**

War is nothing but a continuation of politics with the admixture of other means.

Schopenhauer   **Christopher Janaway**

The word of man is the most durable of all material.

Kierkegaard   **Patrick Gardiner**

An honest religious thinker is like a tightrope walker. He almost looks as though he were walking on nothing but air. His support is the slenderest imaginable. And yet it really is possible to walk on it.

Marx   **Peter Singer**

The philosophers have only interpreted the world in various ways; the point is to change it.

Engels   **Terrell Carver**

Naturally, the workers are perfectly free; the manufacturer does not force them to take his materials and his cards, but he says to them: 'If you don't like to be frizzled in my frying-pan, you can take a walk into the fire.'

Nietzsche   **Michael Tanner**

What I understand by 'philosopher': a terrible explosive in the presence of which everything is in danger.

Russell   **A. C. Grayling**

Every man, wherever he goes, is encompassed by a cloud of comforting convictions, which move with him like flies on a summer day.

Wittgenstein   **A. C. Grayling**

Philosophy is a battle against the bewitchment of our intelligence by means of language.

Heidegger   **Michael Inwood**

Beauty is a fateful gift of the essence of truth, and here truth means the disclosure of what keeps itself concealed.

Forthcoming
Existentialism, Thomas Flynn

Chapter 3
What can the past tell us?

Introduction   **Mary Beard**

A quotation from ancient Rome's most famous poet sits in the pockets and purses, tills and collecting boxes, of most people in Britain. Around the edge of the English one pound coin are engraved three Latin words: 'decus et tutamen', 'an ornament and a protection' – or (as the Bank of England would like you to think) 'something that looks nice and something you can rely on'. This slogan has been a feature of British coinage for hundreds of years. It was apparently suggested by the 17th-century diarist John Evelyn, who claimed to have got it from Cardinal Richelieu. But its first appearance was 2,000 years ago in Virgil's monumental epic poem, the *Aeneid* – his grand re-telling of the story of the foundation of the Eternal City, a classic meditation on the nature of political power and leadership. Halfway through the narrative, the hero Aeneas launches some lavish games to mark the funeral of his father. One of the events is a boat race, and the prize for the man who took second place is a piece of armour, a breast-plate interwoven with gold: 'decus et tutamen' as Virgil put it.

Why on earth the second prize in an ancient rowing competition (the first prize was a rather more splendid cloak) should make its mark so firmly on British coinage is just the kind of question that drives Very Short Introductions. And these ancient echoes are not just a quirk of British culture and coinage. The slogan on the United States' dollar bill – 'e pluribus unum', 'one [state] made out of many' – is itself taken from an even more unlikely ancient source: the recipe for a salad in a poem also thought to have been written by Virgil. The modern Greek two euro piece actually features an image of the frankly misogynistic ancient myth of the rape of Europa, carried off by the god Zeus in the shape of a bull. It makes the starting point for Helen Morales's exciting, fresh look at the uses of classical mythology in the contemporary world, in her forthcoming *Classical Myth: A Very Short Introduction*.

But if the ancient world jangles in all our pockets, it also confronts us from stage and screen, from hoardings and textbooks, novels and posters, low and high art. From the movie *Gladiator* to Freud's Oedipus complex, Very Short Introductions are there to open our eyes. Harry Sidebottom's *Ancient Warfare: A Very Short Introduction*, in fact, starts with those memorable scenes at the beginning of *Gladiator* which recreated a terrible battle between Romans and Germans – and it proceeds to wonder not only how accurate Ridley Scott's movie is as a picture of ancient fighting, but also how such military conflicts between the forces of ruthless 'civilisation' and those of undisciplined 'barbarism' have become a key image in Western culture, from Homer on.

Of course, Greece and Rome are not the only ancient civilisations that exert this pull on our imagination, as the Curse of the Mummy's Tomb and Rosetta Stone t-shirts, tea-towels, and duvet covers vividly remind us. Geraldine Pinch introduces her *Egyptian Myth: A Very Short Introduction* with a close look at the obelisk known as 'Cleopatra's Needle' now on the banks of the Thames – a familiar part of the London street-scene and at the same time a marvellous entry point into the thought world of Egypt. In *Hieroglyphs: A Very Short Introduction* Penelope Wilson lucidly decodes the mysteries of ancient Egyptian writing, before going on to reflect on why they still remain so fascinating. And Ian Shaw's *Ancient Egypt: A Very Short Introduction* not only offers a general introduction to the culture, art, mythology, and religion of Egyptian society, millennia ago – but also examines the impact of Ancient Egypt on our own world. Why are we so ghoulishly fascinated by mummies? Is there a 'Tomb Raider' in all of us?

All these books look at what the ancient world was about and why it still matters to us now.

The heart of the matter

Classics: A Very Short Introduction was the first in the whole series; and, as an inaugural volume, it made clear (or so I like to imagine) that no introduction to anything about the modern world could be complete without an introduction to Classics. We did not set out to write the history of Greece and Rome, or of the 'classics' of Greek and Latin literature that are still read, performed, and enjoyed today (though plenty of that comes in *en route*). Nor was it a question of simply explaining how ancient Greece and Rome have impacted on our own world (though there is some fond discussion of T. S. Eliot, Asterix, Louis MacNeice, and Nigel Molesworth). We wanted to open up all that territory that lies between us and the ancient world itself – the story that goes back beyond the everyday coin of the 21st century, through Evelyn and Richelieu to Virgil himself. And we wanted to show how and why the classical world, along with its inheritance, is still worth arguing about. Mussolini's attempts to re-figure himself as the first Roman emperor Augustus, Karl Marx's training in Greek philosophy, or Freud's reading of Greek myth still matter; as does the hot topic of where, and to whom, the Parthenon marbles belong, or whether Greek democracy offers a useful model for our own beleaguered political systems. If the languages of Greece and Rome are in one sense 'dead', the study of Classics is never a *post mortem*. It lies somewhere at the root of pretty much everything that we can say, see, or think within Western culture. Or so *Classics: A Very Short Introduction* tries to show.

The same could be said of Paul Bahn's *Archaeology: A Very Short Introduction*. He offers a hard look at what remnants of antiquity

What can the past tell us?

archaeologists actually dig out of the ground; but he also presents a wry angle on the arguments that rage on how all this material is to be interpreted. It is an engaging entry-point to the fierce debates between archaeologists the world over on what all the traces of flint and shards of pottery really can tell us about how ancient societies worked and lived. One of the most revealing cartoons in the book (which is illustrated throughout with some hilarious gems from Bill Tidy and others) pictures a group of professional archaeologists in the course of an 'academic argument' (Figure 5): as one of the archaeologists biffs another with a placard reading 'Burn all Neo-Marxist heretics', and another retorts by shouting 'Phallocrat scum-bag', the Joe Public family (who have just come to visit an attractive heritage site on a Sunday afternoon out) retreat in horror and confusion at the scene. Bahn's book is a wonderfully funny – and also informative – attempt to explain what might be going on in these kinds of disputes. What is it that archaeologists discuss in such heated tones? How do they argue about how to make sense of the traces of ancient culture they dig up? And what difference does it make for the rest of us, who might only want to put a name and a date to the scant ruins or the fragments in the museum case?

Anniversary issues

It seems nicely appropriate then that with its 150th book the series should return to the ancient world in Christopher Kelly's *The Roman Empire: A Very Short Introduction*. Not a reign-by-reign survey of despots, madmen, and the occasional benevolent dictator, this is an attempt to think about what really matters for us when we try to understand the biggest imperial power in the West before the 19th century. It is a story of (amongst other things) nationalism, cultural revolution, imperial aggression, and religious conflict. A story of a superpower which is simultaneously frighteningly familiar to us and strangely remote.

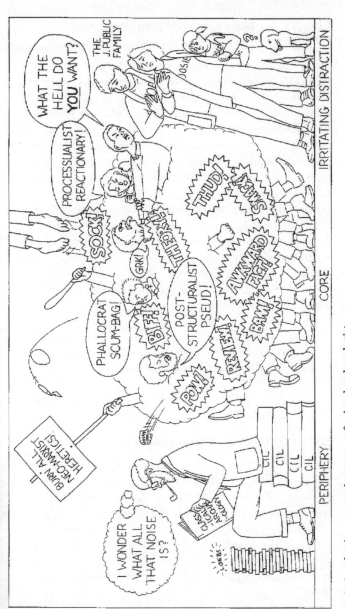

5. An 'academic argument' among professional archaeologists

Classics   **Mary Beard and John Henderson**

Classics can itself be *good to think with* – as well as fun. Again and again, imaginative entertainments and instructive re-creations explore Greek and Roman culture to find orientation for our own world, and to offer opportunities to fantasize. Cleopatras of all sorts – on the page, the stage, or celluloid – from Claudette Colbert to Elizabeth Taylor, have brought the European West a compelling series of visions of the seductions and perversions of the Orient, plus the irresistible formula that ensures that the dominance of Cleopatra over the captivated Mark Anthony is always in the end cancelled out by her death; the story always ends with the restoration of proper political order and male supremacy. On the other hand, in the *Asterix* cartoon-strips the tables are turned on the powerful, as the last remnants in the last corner of a free Gaul magically overpower the legions of Caesar, mock the dull wits and flabby physiques of his officers and soldiers, and in the end return to their 'Arcadian' village to feast and sup as (the myth lies) they always will.

> *'You could not find two better introducers to the Classics than Mary Beard and John Henderson. They are questioning, funny, bold, and widely read in many fields. They could not be dull if they tried.'*
>
>   The Times

Roman Empire   **Christopher Kelly**

The Roman Empire was a remarkable achievement. At its height, in the 2nd century AD, it had a population of around 60 million people spread across 5 million square kilometres (roughly twenty times the area of the United Kingdom). Then the Empire stretched from Hadrian's Wall in drizzle-soaked northern England to the sun-baked banks of the Euphrates in Syria; from the great Rhine-Danube river system, which snaked across the fertile, flat lands of Europe from the Low Countries to the Black

Sea, to the rich plains of the North African coast and the luxuriant gash of the Nile valley in Egypt. The Empire completely encircled the Mediterranean. This was the Romans' internal lake, complacently referred to by its conquerors as *mare nostrum* – 'our sea'.

Shock and Awe

Rome was a warrior state. Its military establishment created its own dynamic. In its rigorous discipline, in the superior quality of its weapons, and in the campaign experience of its troops, the Roman army exploited the advantages of scale and repeated success. Victory yielded huge quantities of booty. In turn, the riches plundered from defeated enemies, supplemented with revenue from provincial taxation, funded the heavy cost of continued conquest. The wealth generated by Rome's wars in the eastern Mediterranean was fabled. In fifty years (from 200–150 BC), the rough equivalent in value of over 30 metric tons of gold was seized. The consolidation of Roman power in Asia Minor and the annexation of Syria meant that even these sums could be exceeded. In 62 BC, the victorious Pompey returned from the East with booty worth nearly seventy commissions; they relied on the personal loyalty of their troops and the threat of violence to enforce their continued active involvement in politics. When Julius Caesar completed his tour of duty in Gaul he refused to stand down, as he was constitutionally required to do. In January 49 BC, at the head of his army of veterans, battle-hardened after eight years of campaigning, he crossed the river Rubicon (which marked the southern territorial limit of his command) and marched on Rome. It was now clear that Caesar's authority rested on military might. Some were prepared to oppose this *coup d'état*, and by equally illegal means. Caesar's assassination five years later on the Ides of March 44 BC need not be seen as a virtuous bid for liberty on the part of Brutus and Cassius. (Shakespeare's version should be put firmly to one side.) It was rather a brutal attempt by one oligarchic faction to wrench political control away from a rival.

Archaeology   **Paul Bahn**

To the general public, archaeology tends to be synonymous with digging, as if this is what practitioners of the subject do all the time. In the British satirical magazine *Private Eye*, any archaeologist is automatically described as 'man with beard in hole'. Cartoons usually depict archaeologists as crusty old fogeys, covered in cobwebs, and obsessed with old bones and cracked pots. Of course, all of this is perfectly accurate, but it only reflects a very small part of the subject. Some archaeologists never excavate, for example, and very few of them spend most of their time at it. Archaeology can provide a window on the last 2.5 million years and help us reconstruct a past that holds a great deal of fascination for us.

Gruesome discoveries

Archaeology can reveal the lives of our distant ancestors, often

6. The mummified body of a man, buried in a peat bog at Lindow, Cheshire

highlighting the trauma and damage their bodies suffered. Many of the preserved bog bodies of northwest Europe clearly met violent deaths, generally as a result of executions, muggings, or ritual sacrifices. Tollund Man was hanged, Grauballe Man had his throat slit, but Britain's Lindow Man – wittily nicknamed Pete Marsh – takes the biscuit: he had his skull fractured twice, was garotted, and had his jugular cut. Either he was extremely unpopular, or someone was determined to do a very thorough job.

> 'a quite brilliant and level-headed look at the curious world of archaeology.'
>
> Barry Cunliffe, University of Oxford

Social and Cultural Anthropology
John Monaghan and Peter Just

Anthropology grew out of the intersection of European discovery, colonialism, and natural science. In the 19th century the first anthropologists, influenced by the same philosophical currents that led to the Darwinian revolution, were interested in reconstructing stages of social and cultural evolution. Influential works were published tracing everything from writing systems to marriage practices from their most primitive origins to their modern manifestations. By the beginning of the last century, anthropologists had developed other intellectual projects and, most importantly, were no longer content to rely on the accounts of colonial officials, missionaries, travellers, and other non-specialists for their primary data. They began to go into the 'field' as ethnographers to gather their own information first hand. Although anthropology has changed quite a bit since the time of these ethnographic pioneers, ethnography remains one of the things that distinguishes anthropology from the rest of the social sciences, and the importance of doing ethnography is perhaps the one thing that all anthropologists agree upon.

Ancient Egypt   **Ian Shaw**

If the attraction of ancient Egyptian culture is its combination of exotica and familiarity, the role of the Egyptologist seems to be to use the available archaeological, visual, and textual sources to

7. **Drawing of the upper part of the Metternich Stela**

distinguish between, on the one hand, aspects of life that are culturally specific either to ourselves or to the ancient Egyptians and, on the other, what Martin Kemp describes as 'a core which has remained fixed and basic since the appearance of the first states in the ancient world'. This is of course not the only reason for studying the civilization of ancient Egypt, although it is this mindset that constantly challenges us to view Egypt not in isolation but as one of many human cultural responses to particular environmental and historical conditions.

Egyptian Myth   **Geraldine Pinch**

For much of the 3rd and 2nd millennia BC, Egypt was the wealthiest and most powerful nation in the Ancient Near East. The Egyptians were pioneers of monumental stone architecture. They produced magnificent sculpture and painted reliefs, and invented the hieroglyphic script, one of the world's earliest and most beautiful forms of writing. Even after Egypt lost its political independence in the late 1st millennium BC, its culture and religion survived to influence those of Greece and Rome.

Mythology was an integral part of Egyptian culture for much of its timespan. Characters and events from myth permeate Egyptian art, architecture, and literature. Myths underpinned many of the rituals performed by kings and priests. Educated Egyptians believed that a knowledge of myth was an essential weapon in the fight to survive the dangers of life and the afterlife.

Ancient Warfare   **Harry Sidebottom**

War was good to think with in the ancient world. In other words, Greeks and Romans frequently used ideas connected to war to understand the world and their place in it. War was used to structure their thoughts on other topics, such as culture, gender, and the individual. War was pervasive in classical thought.

Culture

When Greeks and Romans thought about 'eastern' cultures, and by reflection their own culture, they often did so in terms of warfare. This pattern of thinking was not confined to delineating the oriental. It was a universal practice, although the range of other cultures imagined was limited. For example, when inhabitants of the Roman empire looked to the east, unsurprisingly they saw 'eastern' cultures (depending on their viewpoint Greek, or Persian, and so on). When they turned to the south, again they saw mainly 'eastern' cultures (Carthaginian and Egyptian). To the west was nothing except the ocean, and in it some more or less mythical islands (such as the Islands of the Blest, where a privileged few of the dead lived). It was different up north. The 'northern' was another important imagined 'other' for the classical world. Indeed, before their Romanization, and sometimes in humour afterwards, the inhabitants of the far west, Spaniards, were considered 'northern' in character.

Hieroglyphics   **Penelope Wilson**

The people of Egypt have left behind monuments and objects, many of them covered in the writing now known as Egyptian hieroglyphs. They used this pictorial sign system to write down their language and record aspects of their culture. The information from the writing tells us something about how the Egyptians governed their land and people, about their beliefs, and about their hopes and dreams. Though we can read hieroglyphs this does not mean that we know everything there is to know about Ancient Egypt, partly because the writings have survived accidentally and so are a fraction of the original corpus and partly because the writings only preserve those things the Egyptians themselves thought were important.

This means we have to tread a very careful path in interpreting and attempting to understand the writings, for our sources are biased by chance and by design. They do, however, give us a point of contact with the minds of the Ancient Egyptians.

Chapter 4
Are there any good guys?

Introduction   Stephen Howe

This is a strange, but on the whole a very good, time for anyone interested in history.

The strangeness comes on two very different levels. One is that there seem, in country after country around the globe, to be ever fewer children or young adults who want – or are allowed - to study the subject at schools or universities. History departments shrink or get swallowed up; students migrate to more 'practical' subjects. In some countries' school systems, history no longer exists as a separate subject. In others, teachers complain, it is ever more marginal to the schemes of curriculum planners and educational bureaucrats. The history that *is* studied at school often seems to be a dog's breakfast of ill-assorted themes. In the British school system, it's said with just a touch of exaggeration, it mostly involves repeatedly hearing about the Nazis, and not much else. It is, apparently, not at all a good time to be a *teacher* of history.

The other kind of bewilderment occurs on more rarefied planes. It stems from a pervasive intellectual self-doubt over whether it is, or should be, possible to study history at all. Can we ever have any certain knowledge about what has happened in the past? What, if anything, can it mean to be 'objective', 'unbiased', or 'impartial'? Is there even such a thing as historical 'truth'? Some academic historians start to resemble the proverbial figure of the man busily sawing away at the very branch on which he is sitting. Others again worry that historical studies have become so fragmented into multiple subdisciplines, or so preoccupied with writing about ever more arcane topics for ever smaller, more hyper-specialist readerships, that the subject no longer has any coherence or sense of purpose. It is this mental climate which makes people feel it necessary to write books with titles like *In Defence of History*.

Yet despite and alongside all this, history is massively popular – maybe more so than at any time in the past. History books, including ones of the utmost seriousness, based on massive research, feature regularly in the bestseller lists of almost all countries. History is the only kind of intelligent non-fiction that regularly challenges the popular novel and the lifestyle manual there. Never before has television devoted so much time to historical documentaries and dramas, including numerous digital and satellite channels entirely dedicated to the subject. Family history research is among the most prevalent and still fastest-growing of all leisure pursuits. Millions of people visit historical museums, old buildings, and other 'heritage sites' every weekend. Millions more collect everything from old coins to historic militaria, or decorate and furnish their homes and themselves with different kinds of 'retrochic'. Re-enactment societies vie with local archaeological ones in their apparent omnipresence. All these and many more are manifestations of a genuine mass-based passion for history, however much some scholars may scorn them.

We should also, surely, be impressed by the sheer variety of interests involved. Some people, it's true, are obsessed only with their own family's story – or with legends about it. Most historical research, whether professional or amateur, sticks closely to the writer's own region or country. Most of the history that is formally taught in schools and colleges, in almost every country, is still national in focus. Some commentators seem convinced that people only ever want to read or hear about 'their own kind': Women's History for women only, Black History for black people. . . But the historical fascinations that are revealed in people's spontaneous choice of reading are, encouragingly, far more diverse, less predictable than that (despite those ubiquitous Nazis). Often, it is precisely the most alien or unfamiliar which is most engaging. Ever more readers are curious about a *global* past, not just a local or national one. History Very Short Introductions (VSIs) reflect that breadth and diversity. Alongside a strong list of titles in British history, there are recent books on global themes: Malise Ruthven on *Islam*, John Parker and Richard Rathbone on *African History*, Charles Townshend on *Terrorism*, Steven Grosby's *Nationalism*, Margaret Walters' *Feminism*, or my own *Empire*. Studies of major European thinkers like Quentin Skinner's *Machiavelli* are matched by ones on equally important figures from elsewhere in the world, like Bhikhu Parekh's *Gandhi*. The range is broad in time as well as space, with the ancient and medieval past amply represented as in recent VSIs on *The Celts* (Barry Cunliffe), *The Vikings* (Julian Richards), and *The Crusades* (Christopher Tyerman).

In a quite different register, states and politicians are obviously convinced that history matters, and always have been so convinced. No subject is so intensely political. In countries as diverse as Australia and Israel, Germany and India – just to mention a few of those where bitter disputes are raging right now as I write - competing views about national histories are at the heart of controversy over the very meaning of nationhood. Communities in conflict sustain themselves, and seek to justify their causes, with their rival versions of history – as in modern Ireland and especially the North, subject of VSIs by Senia Paseta and Marc Mulholland. Not only does the study of history almost always carry a powerful political and moral charge, but the very concept of *Politics*, or of such key values as *Democracy*, can only be understood historically: Kenneth Minogue's and Bernard Crick's VSIs on those themes make that point with both force and verve.

History, then, is quite generally felt to carry both moral and political authority. Yet its appeal is not just on so deadly serious a level. People turn to historians wanting to learn, to seek guidance about burning contemporary issues and perennial puzzles of the human heart. But they also seek entertainment, and no serious intellectual field has such innate potential to entertain as history does. Its capacity to surprise, to offer the 'shock of the new' by looking with fresh eyes at the old, is almost unlimited. Things you thought you knew, ideas you thought you understood, are shaken up. New patterns emerge, new ways of seeing are revealed. Personally, I have found myself pleasurably startled out of my previous assumptions by VSIs on subjects with which I'd thought I was almost wearily familiar, like Kevin Passmore's on *Fascism*, Colin Ward's on *Anarchism*, or John Pinder's on the *European Union*.

Many historians (though sadly, by no means all) actually take care over how they write, avoid obscurantism and pointless jargon, make the effort to be accessible, enjoyable, even amusing as well as soberly reflective. Certainly the authors of all the history VSIs do all those things. They all try strenuously to avoid both jargon and cliché – and the choice of illustrations is often enjoyably unexpected and cliché-free too. (The proudest boast of my own *Empire* VSI is that, almost uniquely among works on its subject, it contains no pictures of lions at all.)

History students are, very early in their studies, routinely admonished that they should avoid narrative, and go for an analytical approach instead. But a great deal of history's appeal lies precisely in the sphere of narrative, and there is no reason to be snobbish about that. There is nothing intellectually disreputable about telling stories. It is among the oldest of all human activities, one of the most universal, one of the most demanding. So several of the history VSIs – like the splendid series which now covers almost the entire sweep of British history, from Peter Salway's *Roman Britain* to Kenneth Morgan on the twentieth century, or like William Doyle and S. A. Smith on the French and Russian Revolutions – offer clear, vigorous narratives, telling us what happened, to whom, and when. John Arnold's *History* VSI itself urges the point that history is, at bottom, about individuals, what they did and what was done to them – and Arnold illustrates this with some dazzling vignettes of his own. But of course 'narrative' and 'analysis' are not really opposites nor enemies. All these books offer something more than a good story well told. They work hard at explaining why things happened, or why people believed what they did – or for that matter, where necessary, why historians can't agree about such issues. These volumes may be 'Introductions', but they are not 'Idiot's Guides'. All of them reflect and try to summarise many years' hard thinking on their subjects by the authors. And they invite the reader to think hard about them too.

History   John H. Arnold

Do historians reconstruct the truth or simply tell stories? John Arnold suggests that they do both, and that the balance between 'truth' and 'story' is tremendously important to history. Taking us from the fabulous tales of ancient Greek historians to the varied approaches of modern historians, he illuminates our relationship to the past by making us aware of how 'history' has changed as a subject. Concepts such as periodization and causation are discussed through particular historical examples that illustrate the ways in which we understand history, giving the reader a sense of the excitement of discovering not only the past, but also something about ourselves.

Evidence and interpretation

Historians, like everyone else, can misread, misremember, misinterpret, or misunderstand things. Every historical account has gaps, problems, contradictions, areas of uncertainty. An author of fiction can invent people, places, and happenings, whereas a historian is bound by what the evidence will support. For every historian, what is at stake is what actually happened – and what it might *mean*. There is an excitement to these precarious attempts to grasp the 'truth', a truth that might at any point be revealed as illusory.

> *'His range of knowledge and interests is phenomenal, but his skill as a communicator makes his own subtle analysis of history's history as gripping as a novel.'*
>
> Neal Ascherson

Prehistory **Chris Gosden**

A prehistoric site

The activities of a group of early people and animals at Boxgrove, near Chichester in southern England, half a million years ago can be reconstructed using archaeology. None of the creatures involved had the remotest awareness that traces of their activities would survive for half a million years, preserved by rapid burial under collapsing cliff sediments. No words survive to tell us of this and countless other incidents, but we can give voice to questions aplenty. Beautifully detailed excavation and recording of the site has shown six (or perhaps seven) discrete areas of flint working where hand axes were fashioned. Dealing with a three-dimensional jigsaw puzzle, archaeologists have worked in reverse order to the earlier hominids – rather than breaking down a big nodule of flint into small flakes and a large hand axe, they have put the flakes back together again to create a complete nodule with only one missing element, the hand axe itself. A void is left in the centre of the stone, reminding us that in some parts of the world more recent stone knappers have seen their task as not making a stone tool, but rather freeing it from its encasing stone material. Once freed, these particular hand axes have so far eluded archaeological detection, although they may lie in another part of the same site, discarded by a meat-bloated creature moving off to rest somewhere safe. Indeed, many dozens of near-pristine hand axes have been recovered from Boxgrove, some with microscopic traces that indicate they were used for butchery.

Vikings **Julian D. Richards**

The Viking reputation is of bloodthirsty seafaring warriors, repeatedly plundering the British Isles and the North Atlantic throughout the early Middle Ages. Yet Vikings were also traders, settlers, and farmers, with a complex artistic and linguistic culture.

The term *viking* was first used in Old English. It occurs just three times in the Anglo-Saxon Chronicle where it refers to 'robbers', apparently coastal marauders rather than land-borne armies. It was not used in other countries which suffered raids from Scandinavia, and Western observers gave the raiders many different names. In some cases it was their religion, or lack of it, that was significant, and they were referred to as pagans, heathen, or gentiles. In the Irish Annals they were often seen as just different and were called *gaill*, or 'foreigners'. In other contexts it was where they came from that was of interest, and they were *Northmanni*, or *Dani*, although such labels were often used indiscriminately, irrespective of their actual area of origin. Finally, it may have been their function that stood out, as *pirate* or *scipmen*.

The Celts   **Barry Cunliffe**

At the beginning of the 21st century the Celtic debate is in full flood, with all shades of opinion being expressed – in the title of a 1998 article by Patrick Sims Williams – 'from celtomania to celtoscepticism'. The debate is lively and sometimes a little bad-tempered, but what all contestants will agree on is the intriguing complexity of the subject. There are many strands of very disparate data to be examined. The direct archaeological evidence contributes insights into ritual behaviour, burial practices, settlement layouts, and a wide array of material culture including distinctive art styles commonly referred to as Celtic Art. Linguistic studies show something of the extent, development, and survival of the group of closely related languages which, after Lhuyd, we still call Celtic. Then there are the Classical sources – Greek and Roman writers with their references to *Celti, Celtae, Keltoi, Celtici, Galli, Gallici*, and *Galatae* – curious barbarians to be caricatured and used as local colour in the many 'histories' presenting the interactions and conflicts from which the Graeco-Roman world would, through the craft of the writer, emerge triumphant.

Nor can we overlook the potential contribution of the rich vernacular literature of Ireland and Wales and the ancient Law tracts of these countries – texts built up from ancient oral traditions modified over generations and layered with accretions at each retelling.

It is a rich mix of ingredients, but what we cannot do is to fling them all into one pot and expect a perfectly formed Celt to emerge. Each of the different categories of evidence has to be considered within its own critical parameters to separate fact from wishful thinking and to distil out what it has to offer to the debate. Whether, in this process of deconstruction, Celts and Celticism will vanish altogether remains to be seen. To find out, read on.

The Crusades   Christopher Tyerman

The word 'crusade', a non-medieval Franco-Spanish hybrid only popularized in English since the 18th century, has entered the Anglo-American language as a synonym for a good cause vigorously pursued, from pacific Christian evangelism to militant temperance. However floridly and misleadingly romantic, the image of mailed knights bearing crosses on surcoats and banners, fighting for their faith under an alien sun, occupies a familiar niche in the façade of modern western perceptions of the past. Despite, or perhaps because of, its lack of context, it remains the indelible image of crusading in popular culture, shared even by the sculptors of the late President Assad of Syria. Iconography is never innocent. Assad's Damascus Saladin is defeating the Christians at their own imperialist game as surely as the Ladybird's Saladin and Richard I are playing out some 19th-century cultural minuet. Polemicists and politicians know – or should know – that to invoke the Crusades is to stir deep cultural myths, assumptions, and prejudices, a fact recognized by Pope John Paul II's apology to Jews, Muslims, and

Eastern Orthodox Christians for the intolerance and violence inflicted by Catholic warriors of the cross. Although it is difficult to see how even Christ's Vicar on earth can apologize for events in which he did not participate, over which he had no control, and for which he bore no responsibility, this intellectually muddled gesture acknowledged the continued inherent potency of crusading, a story that can still move, outrage, and inflame. One of the groups led by the fundamentalist religious terrorist Usama bin Laden was known as 'The World Islamic Front for Crusade against Jews and Crusaders'. To understand medieval crusading for itself and to explain its survival may be regarded as an urgent contemporary task, one for which historians must take responsibility. To this dual study of history and historiography, of the Crusades and what could be called their post-history, this is a brief introduction.

The Renaissance   Jerry Brotton

In Western Europe, the word 'Renaissance' immediately conjures up images of places like Florence and Venice, and the great artists and thinkers of the 15th and 16th centuries – Leonardo, Michelangelo, Copernicus, and Shakespeare. It's an intoxicating and deeply persuasive idea that has held sway for nearly two centuries. This book challenges these deeply held assumptions by arguing that they were invented in the 19th century by a group of historians who had little interest in the more global and multicultural influences that actually underpinned the foundations of the Renaissance. In fact, the very term 'renaissance' was invented by historians like Jules Michelet and Jacob Burckhardt in the 19th century; nobody in the 15th century would have identified themselves as living through a 'renaissance' in the way that we see ourselves as living in the 'modern world'.

Rather than Florence, Rome, and Venice, it was places to the east of Europe – Constantinople, Baghdad, Cairo, Damascus, and the bazaars of North Africa and the Middle East – that made crucial contributions to the Renaissance world. The wealth of luxury objects that Europe bought from the east – spices, silk, porcelain, gems, horses, even pigments for painting – all contributed to the extraordinary transformation in art, taste, and cultural life that we now call the European Renaissance. As well as objects, new ideas in science and the arts were openly and amicably exchanged with Arabic and Islamic cultures to Europe's east. Developments in algebra, astronomy, anatomy, finance, even the word for 'cheque', all resulted from European merchants and artists travelling to the east and learning new ideas, which were slowly but profoundly absorbed into the European way of life.

> 'A young Turk who likes to entertain ... This is a Renaissance you can touch and feel'
>
> Sunday Times

British history in VSIs

Roman Britain   Peter Salway

Britain was within the orbit of Graeco-Roman civilization for at least half a millennium, and for over 350 years was part of the political union created by the Roman Empire that encompassed most of Europe and all the countries of the Mediterranean. Here, the author weaves together the results of archaeological investigation and historical scholarship to chart the history of Britain from the first invasion under Julius Caesar to the final collapse of the Romano-British way of life in the 5th century AD.

> 'Highly readable, attractively illustrated, admirably succinct, yet with the odd surprise even for the comparatively well-informed.'
>
> The Scotsman

The Anglo-Saxon Age   John Blair

Covering the period from the earliest English settlements to the Norman victory in 1066, this book is a brief introduction to the political, social, religious, and cultural history of an age when so many basic aspects of modern England were formed: its language, governmental institutions, rural landscape, communications, and towns.

Medieval Britain John Gillingham and Ralph A. Griffiths

The establishment of the Anglo-Norman monarchy in the early Middle Ages, through to England's failure to dominate the British Isles and France in the later Middle Ages, provide the historical markers for this analysis of Medieval Britain. Out of the turbulence came stronger senses of identity in Scotland, Wales, and Ireland. Yet this was an age, too, of growing definition of Englishness and of a distinctive English cultural tradition.

The Tudors John Guy

The most authoritative short introduction to this exciting long century, *The Tudors* offers a compelling account of the political, religious, and economic changes in Britain under such leading monarchs as Henry VIII and Elizabeth I. This Very Short Introduction also provides a comprehensive reassessment of the reigns of Henry VII, Edward VI, and Philip and Mary.

Stuart Britain John Morrill

A century of revolution is here set into its political, religious, social, economic, intellectual, and cultural contexts. This title describes the effects of a period during which population was growing inexorably, faster than both the food supply and the employment market. Morrill also portrays the unexpected irruption into civil war which then took on a terrifying momentum of its own, resulting in violent revolution and in the abolition of the monarchy, the House of Lords, and the established Church. He goes on to describe how painfully and with what difficulty order and obedience were restored.

Eighteenth-Century Britain   Paul Langford

Eighteenth-century Britain is sometimes thought of as sedate, oligarchical, and conservative. Langford reveals the essential vitality as Britain evolved into a great power, an industrial giant, and a dynamic commercial society. The transforming effect of 100 years is concisely narrated in all its diversity and complexity.

Nineteenth-Century Britain   Christopher Harvie and H. C. G. Matthew

A sharp but subtle account of remarkable economic and social change – and an even more remarkable political stability. Britain in 1789 was overwhelmingly rural, agrarian, multilingual, and almost half Celtic. By 1914, when it faced its greatest test since the defeat of Napoleon, it was largely urban and English. The authors highlight the forces behind Britain's rise to its imperial zenith, and the continuing tensions within the nations of the 'union state'.

Twentieth-Century Britain   Kenneth O. Morgan

The forces of consensus and of conflict in 20th-century Britain are discussed in this wide-ranging yet concise analysis of the last century. Morgan covers the trauma of the First World War and the social divisions of the 1920s; fierce domestic and foreign policy debates in the 1930s; the impact of the Second World War on domestic transformation, popular culture, and the loss of empire; the transition from the turmoil of the 1970s to the aftermath of Thatcherism and the advent of New Labour. Profound tensions that shook the United Kingdom are juxtaposed against an equally deep desire for stability, cohesion, and a sense of historic identity.

Empire   Stephen Howe

A great deal of the world's history is the history of empires. Howe explores the idea of empire in the widest sense, from the ancient

Roman Empire, through the colonization of the Americas and the Soviet empire, to our recent memories of colonial rule and the new economic-based imperial systems. This is a challenging and compelling book that offers new insights into profound changes in the modern world.

Writers on empire

> The conquest of the earth, which mostly means the taking it away from those who have a different complexion or slightly flatter noses than ourselves, is not a pretty thing when you look at it too much. What redeems it is the idea only. An idea at the back of it; not a sentimental pretence but an idea; an unselfish belief in the idea – something you can set up, and bow down before, and offer a sacrifice to.

> Joseph Conrad in *Heart of Darkness* (1899)

> And it was at this moment, as I stood there with the rifle in my hands, that I first grasped the hollowness, the futility of the white man's dominion in the East. Here was I, the white man with his gun, standing in front of the unarmed native crowd – seemingly the leading actor in the piece; but in reality I was only an absurd puppet pushed to and fro by the will of those yellow faces behind. I perceived in this moment that when the white man turns tyrant it is his own freedom that he destroys. He becomes a sort of hollow, posturing dummy, the conventionalized figure of a sahib. For it is a condition of his rule, that he shall spend his life in trying to impress the 'natives' and so in every crisis he has got to do what the 'natives' expect of him. He wears a mask, and his face grows to fit it.

> George Orwell in 'Shooting an Elephant' (1936)

Globalization   Manfred Steger

'Globalization studies' is emerging as a new field that cuts across traditional disciplinary boundaries. This strong emphasis on interdisciplinarity requires students of globalization to familiarize

	Country	GDP ($ mil)	Corporation	Sales ($ mil)
	Country	**GDP ($ mil)**	**Corporation**	**Sales ($ mil)**
1.	Denmark	174,363.0	General Motors	176,558.0
2.	Poland	154,146.0	Wal-Mart	166,809.0
3.	South Africa	131,127.0	Exxon Mobil	163,881.0
4.	Israel	99,068.0	Royal Dutch/Shell	105,366.0
5.	Ireland	84,861.0	IBM	87,548.0
6.	Malaysia	74,634.0	Siemens	75,337.0
7.	Chile	71,092.0	Hitachi	71,858.5
8.	Pakistan	59,880.0	Sony	60,052.7
9.	New Zealand	53,622.0	Honda Motor	54,773.5
10.	Hungary	48,355.0	Credit Suisse	49,362.0

Countries versus transnational corporations: A comparison

SOURCE: Sales: *Fortune*, 31 July 2000. GDP: World Bank, *World Development Report 2000*.

themselves with literatures on subjects that have often been studied in isolation from each other. The greatest challenge facing today's globalization researcher lies, therefore, in connecting and synthesizing the various strands of knowledge in a way that does justice to the increasingly fluid and interdependent nature of our postmodern world. In short, globalization studies calls for an interdisciplinary approach broad enough to behold the 'big picture'. Such a comprehensive intellectual enterprise may well lead to the rehabilitation of the academic generalist whose status, for too long, has been overshadowed by the specialist.

The author argues that we should take comfort in the fact that the world is becoming a more interdependent place that enhances people's ability to recognize and acknowledge their common humanity.

The French Revolution   **William Doyle**

Every person of good general knowledge in the 19th century knew something about the great upheaval that had marked the last years of the 18th. Nobody who knew anything of France, even at second hand (if only through learning what was still the first foreign language of choice throughout most of the world), could fail to imbibe some sense that this country had been marked by a traumatic convulsion only just beyond living memory. Many believed, or felt, that this must have been for the best and somehow necessary. New nations have been proud to proclaim their emancipation, or to anticipate it, like the patriots of Brussels in 1789, or Milan in 1796, by adopting tricolour flags. This banner of liberty still flies from Rome to Mexico City, from Bucharest to Dublin. Poles, who first sang the *Marseillaise* in 1794 as they resisted the carve-up of their country, sang it again in 1956 in revolt against Soviet tyranny. In 1989, as France commemorated the Revolution's 200th anniversary, the same anthem of defiance was heard in Beijing, among the doomed student protesters in Tiananmen Square. Few countries have failed to experience some sort of revolution since 1789, and in all of them there have been people looking back to what happened in France then and subsequently for inspiration, models, patterns, or warnings.

> *'The best introduction to its subject in any language'*
> Tim Blanning, University of Cambridge

The Russian Revolution   S. A. Smith

The years between 1918 and 1922 in Russia witnessed a level of strife and anarchy unparalleled since the 'Time of Troubles' of 1605–13, when struggles between pretenders to the throne brought Russia to a state of chaos. The civil war brutalized social life to an unimaginable degree, yet as an epic struggle between the new and old worlds it inspired idealism and heroism among the dedicated minorities who supported the Red and White causes. The young Bolshevik V. Poliansky recalled:

> We all lived in an atmosphere of revolutionary romanticism, tired, exhausted, but joyful, festive, our hair uncut, unwashed, unshaven, but bright and clear in heart and mind.

Yet the reality was that Russia succumbed to an economic and social cataclysm. The population on Soviet territory fell by 12.7 million between 1917 and early 1922, only partly due to civil war as such. The losses of Soviet armed forces ranged from 1,150,000 to 1,250,000; and, when the losses of Whites, partisans, and nationalist forces are included, war-related losses rise to between 2.5 million and 3.3 million. Far more perished as a result of disease – between 1917 and 1920 over 2 million died of typhus, typhoid fever, smallpox, and dysentery – causing Lenin to warn that, 'either the louse will defeat socialism or socialism will defeat the louse'. Finally, and most hideously, between 1921 and 1922 as many as 6 million died of starvation and disease in a famine that devastated the Volga region and Ukraine. Not without reason did the novelist Boris Pasternak conclude: 'In our days even the air smells of death.'

The First World War   Michael Howard

If there was a single political cause for the war, it was the advent among the European powers of a dynamic new German Empire whose combination of military, economic, and industrial strength seemed, to its ruling classes, to entitle it to a ranking among world powers that it did not as yet possess. At the same time it appeared threatened by a domestic instability that made its rulers apprehensive as well as ambitious. Simultaneously, the growth of nationalism among the Slav peoples of Central and Southeast Europe threatened the survival of Germany's ally, the multi-national Habsburg Empire. In both countries war increasingly seemed the only solution to their problems, but this mood was general not only in Vienna and Berlin. Throughout Europe there was a sense that war would be a necessary therapy for a society that urbanization, secularization, and modernization were making degenerate and decadent. Rupert Brooke was not the only poet who felt like 'a swimmer into cleanness leaping' when Britain declared war on 14 August 1914.

Those primarily concerned with planning the war knew that unless it could be rapidly won its consequences would be terrible. They hoped that, like its predecessors of 1866 and 1870, it could be settled in a few great battles, leaving the framework of society undisturbed. There were indeed great battles, notably those of Tannenberg and the Marne, but they settled nothing. Belligerent governments summoned up reserves of man-power, converted their industries to the production of munitions, found financial resources from loans, taxes, or simply inflation, and settled down to a war of attrition. This involved wearing down not only each other's armies but their entire societies to the point of collapse; killing their soldiers and starving their civilians. The greater the sacrifices they suffered, the more reluctant they were to consider any peace short of total victory.

'succinct, comprehensive and beautifully written'
Times Literary Supplement

The Spanish Civil War   Helen Graham

The Spanish Civil War was the first fought in Europe in which civilians became targets *en masse*, through bombing raids on big cities. The new photo-journalism that made Spain's the first 'photogenic' war in history also transmitted searing images of the vast numbers of political refugees produced by the conflict. There had been mass population displacements during the First World War, but none had had Spain's visibility. The Civil War made a deep impression on those watching from other European countries. For Spaniards themselves, the shock was huge. There were no remotely comparative terms of reference for the military, industrial, social, and political mobilization the Civil War produced, since Spain had not participated in the First World War of 1914–18. As is well known, Spain also became the place where other powers tested the latest technologies of warfare. Even more bleakly, the conflict revealed what war on European soil could mean – presaging the purificatory, genocidal, and retributive conflicts of those many other civil wars waged across the continent between 1939 and the end of the 1940s.

Fascism   **Kevin Passmore**

Nazi Germany: The Enabling Act 1933

The opening session of the last Reichstag took place in the Kroll Opera House, situated on the Tiergarten in central Berlin, for the Reichstag building had been destroyed by fire a few weeks previously. Inside the hall a huge swastika flag hung behind the platform occupied by the cabinet and President of the Reichstag. Only one item lay before the Reichstag: an Enabling Law, giving the Chancellor the power to issue laws without the approval of the Reichstag, even where they deviated from the constitution. Frowning intensely, Hitler read his declaration with an unusual self-possession. In reply, the socialist Otto Wels courageously invoked the 'principles of humanity and justice, of freedom and socialism'. Yet the French Ambassador remembered that he spoke with the air of a beaten child. His voice choking with emotion, Wels concluded by expressing best wishes to those already filling concentration camps and prisons. Hitler responded by accusing socialists of having persecuted the Nazis for 14 years. Socialists heckled, but stormtroopers behind them hissed 'you'll be strung up today'.

The Enabling Law was passed by 444 votes against the 94 of the socialists. It destroyed the rule of law and in practice licensed the Nazis to act as they saw fit, in the 'higher interests of the German people', against anyone deemed to be an enemy of the Reich.

> 'excellent introduction ... concise and refreshingly free of jargon.'
>
> Times Literary Supplement

The Cold War　**Robert McMahon**

The vast swath of death and destruction precipitated by the
Second World War left not only much of Europe and Asia in ruins
but the old international order as well. 'The whole world structure
and order that we had inherited from the nineteenth century was
gone', marvelled US Assistant Secretary of State Dean Acheson.
Indeed, the Eurocentric international system that had dominated
world affairs for the past 500 years had, virtually overnight,
vanished. Two continent-sized military behemoths – already being
dubbed superpowers – had risen in its stead, each intent upon
forging a new order consonant with its particular needs and
values. As the war moved into its final phase, even the most casual
observer of world politics could see that the United States and the
Soviet Union held most of the military, economic, and diplomatic
cards. On one basic goal, those adversaries-turned-allies were in
essential accord: that some semblance of authority and stability
needed to be restored with dispatch – and not just to those areas
directly affected by the war but to the broader international
system as well. The task was as urgent as it was daunting since, as
Under Secretary of State Joseph Grew warned in June 1945:
'Anarchy may result from the present economic distress and
political unrest.'

Modern Ireland　**Senia Pašeta**

The Act of Union between Great Britain and Ireland which came
into effect on 1 January 1801 presents historians with a convenient
but far from straightforward starting point for a survey of modern
Irish history. Many of the conflicts which have characterized Irish
political, social, and economic life since 1800 were in place well
before the Act was introduced. International events were already
exacerbating local tensions. The violent and dynamic final three
decades of the 18th century which prompted the introduction of the
Act were themselves products of a longer and constantly evolving
struggle between competing political minds, identities, and

programmes. The Act of Union attempted to address the issues underlying the conflicts, but each one continued to simmer throughout the next two centuries.

Northern Ireland   Marc Mulholland

Bloody Sunday, on 30 January 1972, was the debacle that led to the almost complete collapse of Catholic opposition to political violence. Confronting a relatively small-scale riot, the elite parachute regiment shot dead 13 unarmed demonstrators (a 14th died later of wounds). One British Army officer indicated perfectly the self-defeating militarism of counter-insurgency: 'When we moved on the streets we moved as if we in fact were moving against a well-armed, well-trained army.' Not one of the fatalities on Bloody Sunday was an IRA man. Had the British Army fired on a similar crowd a month later, again targeting men of military age, they would hardly have been able to avoid enemy kills: Bloody Sunday led to a mass influx into the ranks of the Derry IRA. The relentless bombing campaign was accelerated; of the city's 150 shops, only 20 were left trading. Almost one-third of the 320 deaths in Derry attributed to the Troubles were the result of street clashes and gun battles during this period (54 of those killed were members of the Security Forces).

Terrorism   Charles Townshend

Terrorism upsets people. It does so deliberately. That is its point, and that is why it has engaged so much of our attention at the turn of the 21st century. The 11 September 2001 attack on New York saw damage that looked like a wartime air raid. Although the casualty list mercifully shrank from a potential 50,000 to 5,000, and finally to less than 4,000, the vision of mass destruction, previously restricted to the kind of weapons possessed by only a handful of major powers, had appeared.

The search for an 'adequate' definition of terrorism is still on. Why the difficulty? In a word, it is 'labelling', because 'terrorist' is a description that has almost never been voluntarily adopted by any individual or group, possibly as a result of the notion that one person's terrorist is another's freedom fighter. It is applied to them by others, first and foremost by the governments of the states they attack. Terrorism appears to be a state of mind rather than an activity.

What is terrorism?

'The calculated use or threat of violence to inculcate fear, intended to coerce or intimidate governments or societies.'

US Government

'The use or threat, for the purpose of advancing a political, religious or ideological course of action, of serious violence against any person or property.'

UK Government

'Terrorism is a distinctive form of modern political agency, intended to threaten the ability of a state to ensure the security of its members.'

Sunil Khilnani, Professor of Politics, UCL

'Like the other excellent books in this series, this is rigorous and compelling . . . balanced, sensible.'

Independent on Sunday

Nationalism   Steve Grosby

Distinctive of nationalism is the belief that the nation is the only goal worthy of pursuit – an assertion that often leads to the belief that the nation demands unquestioned and uncompromising loyalty. When such a belief about the nation becomes predominant, it can threaten individual liberty. Moreover, nationalism often asserts that other nations are implacable enemies to one's own nation; it injects hatred of what is perceived to be foreign, whether another nation, an immigrant, or a person who may practise another religion or speak a different language. Of course, one need not view one's own nation and its relation to other nations in such a manner.

However, clarifying further what we mean by the terms 'nation' and 'nationalism', and addressing the other questions already raised briefly, involve other related problems: what is a social relation?; what is a territory?; what is kinship?; the appearance of the nation in history; the relation of the nation to religion; and the tendency of humanity to divide itself into different nations. Each of these problems will be taken up in this *Very Short Introduction*.

Anarchism   Colin Ward

Anarchism is a social and political ideology which, despite a history of defeat, continually re-emerges in a new guise or in a new country, so that another chapter has to be added to its chronology, or another dimension to its scope.

The word 'anarchy' comes from the Greek *anarkhia*, meaning contrary to authority or without a ruler, and was used in a derogatory sense until 1840, when it was adopted by Pierre-Joseph Proudhon to describe his political and social ideology. Proudhon argued that organization without government was both possible and desirable. In the evolution of political ideas, anarchism can be seen as an ultimate projection of both liberalism and socialism, and the differing strands of anarchist thought can be related to their emphasis on one or the other of these.

Feminism   Margaret Walters

But how often, still, do we hear women anxiously asserting 'I'm not a feminist but . . .' as they go on to make claims that depend upon, and would be impossible without, a feminist groundwork? The American feminist Estelle Freedman argues that right from its origins, the word has carried negative connotations; that surprisingly few politically engaged women have styled themselves feminists. In the 1990s some feminists in England and the United States identified and warned against a 'backlash' against feminism and its undoubted achievements. Juliet Mitchell and Ann Oakley, for example, called their third collection of essays *Who's Afraid of Feminism?*, with a cartoon of a big bad wolf on the original jacket cover. They argued that 'attacks on feminism frequently merge into a wider misogyny'; 'the feminist' is now the name given to the disliked or despised woman, much as 'man-hater' or 'castrating bitch', 'harridan' or 'witch', were used before the 1960s. They added that women also have to expose and eradicate the misogyny inherent in feminism itself.

Ideology   Michael Freeden

Ideology is one of the most controversial terms in our political vocabulary, exciting both repulsion and inspiration.

In effect, the study of ideology is most profitably recognized as the study of actual political thought – the concrete thinking *of* political communities and *within* political communities. For anyone interested in the sphere of politics that study is not an optional extra; it focuses on the world of ideas and symbols through which political actors find their way and comprehend their social surroundings. It informs their practices and institutions and it establishes the parameters of their moral prescriptions and expectations. It may or may not be illusory; it may or may not represent something else outside it – but *initially* it doesn't really matter that much if what we want to do is to understand what political thinking is, long before we deconstruct it critically or expose its pretensions. To explore ideologies is to penetrate the heart of politics, and it requires a sympathetic student, not a dismissive or a disillusioned one. Politics is principally concerned with making collective decisions and with the regulation of conflict that both precedes and follows such decisions. Thinking about politics is always thinking defined by, and channelled in, those directions.

Socialism   **Michael Newman**

What is socialism? Does it have a future, or has it become an outdated ideology in the 21st century?

Michael Newman examines and explains the successes and failures of modern socialism by taking an international perspective – ranging from communism in Cuba to social democracy in Sweden.

Discussing its evolution from the industrial towns of the 19th century to its response to the feminist, Green, and anti-capitalist movements today, Newman concludes that, with its values of equality, solidarity, and cooperation, socialism remains as relevant as ever but that it needs to learn lessons from the past.

Sociology   **Steve Bruce**

It is a sign of the power of sociology that it is both popular and reviled. Longer established academic disciplines deride it as a gauche newcomer but adopt its perspectives. Ordinary people mock those who pursue it professionally, yet take some of its assumptions for granted. Governments accuse the discipline of undermining morality and social discipline, yet hire sociologists to evaluate their policies.

Our uneasiness with the discipline can be seen in the frequency and the nature of the jokes. This may just be my professional paranoia, but it seems that there are sociologist jokes in a way that there are not historian jokes. As such humour does not translate terribly well I will recount just one. This gem came from the British television series *Minder*, a fine 1980s comedy of minor villains and London low life. Two lovable rogues are discussing a mutual acquaintance who has just been released from prison. One announces that their friend has been improving himself while inside by studying: 'Yeh. He's got an Open University degree now. In sociology.' The second asks: 'Has he given up the thieving then?' and the first replies: 'Nah! But now he knows why he does it!'

Capitalism   **James Fulcher**

Capitalists existed before capitalism proper. Since the earliest times merchants have made money by investing in goods that they sold at a profit. As we saw with the East India Company, a merchant capitalism of this kind could be highly organized and very profitable, but it was an activity that involved only a small part of the economy. Most people's livelihoods did not come from economic activities financed by the investment of capital. In capitalism proper the whole economy becomes dependent on the investment of capital and this occurs when it is not just trade that is financed in this way but production as well.

In a capitalist society, both capital and labour have an abstract and disembedded quality, since both are separated from specific economic activities and are therefore able in principle to move into any activity that suitably rewards them. In real life this mobility is constrained by the existing skills and experience of both the owners of capital and workers, and by the relationships and attachments that they have formed. The potential mobility of capital and labour is, nonetheless, one of the features of capitalist societies that gives them their characteristic dynamism.

So, the answer to the question 'what is capitalism?' is that capitalism involves the investment of money to make more money.

While merchants have long done this, it is when production is financed in this way that a transformative capitalism comes into being. Capitalist production depends on the exploitation of wage labour, which also fuels the consumption of the goods and services produced by capitalist enterprises. Production and consumption are linked by the markets that come to mediate all economic activities. Markets enable competition between enterprises but also generate tendencies towards concentration in order to reduce uncertainty. Market fluctuations also provide the basis of a speculative form of capitalism, which may not be productive but is, nonetheless, based on mechanisms that are central to the operation of a capitalist economy.

Democracy   **Bernard Crick**

No political concept is more used and misused than that of democracy. Here, Crick examines the history of the doctrine, practices, and institutions of democracy. There are many meanings attached to the word 'democracy'; it is what philosophers have called 'an essentially contested concept' because the very definition carries a different social, moral, or political agenda. Plato detested the concept of democracy, considering it to be the rule of opinion over knowledge. Whereas for his pupil, Aristotle, democracy was a basic condition for good government.

Politics   **Kenneth Minogue**

Politics is so central to our civilization that its meaning changes with every change of culture and circumstance. For this reason, our first move in trying to understand politics must be to free ourselves from the unreflective beliefs of the present. One aim of this book is to explain how it came about that what used to be a limited activity conducted by the elites of some Western countries is now thought to be the inescapable preoccupation of mankind. Why do we need politics? If men were angels, no government would be needed. But since some sort of government *is* needed, could we not find a better

solution than the states revealed to us by history as riddled with
war, poverty, and violence? High hopes of this kind have often
erupted among the poor on the margins of politics, and have
sometimes captured the centre. Such hopes unmistakably derive
from a millennial version of Christianity, and they have had
explosive consequences.

British Politics   Tony Wright

Try this game. You have to fill in the blank.

French wine
Italian food
German cars
British __

Not easy, is it? One suggestion might be 'language', which would be
the obvious candidate except for the fact that it is not *English* but
British that we are talking about (a characteristic confusion that is
discussed in this book). This also disqualifies 'hooligans'.

There is a good case to be made for 'politics' or 'government'. This is
not an original answer. Indeed, it has long been held (not least by
the British) that Britain has displayed a particular approach to
politics that has offered lessons to the world in making government
work. 'This country's distinctive contribution to civilisation',
proclaimed the *Daily Telegraph* not so long ago, 'has been the
development of stable institutions of representative government.'
There is plenty to unpick in such a statement (which country
precisely?; what kind of stability?; does representative mean
democratic?), but it faithfully echoes a long line of such judgements
about the political genius and blessings of the British.

The European Union   John Pinder

The European Union of today is the result of a process that began
half a century ago with the creation of the European Coal and Steel

Community. Those two industries then provided the industrial muscle for military power; and Robert Schuman, the French Foreign Minister, affirmed on 9 May 1950, in his declaration to launch the project, that 'any war between France and Germany' would become 'not merely unthinkable, but materially impossible'. The Union has the capacity to provide the framework for Europe's new economy and democratic stability, and to assist the development of a world system that can deliver security and sustainable development.

It may not be easy, at today's distance, to appreciate how much this meant, only five years after the end of the war of 1939–45 which had brought such terrible suffering to almost all European countries. For France and Germany, which had been at war with each other three times in the preceding eight decades, finding a way to live together in a durable peace was a fundamental political priority that the new Community was designed to serve. John Pinder shows us how and why the Union was set up, and how it has developed.

'Invaluable'   The Observer

The World Trade Organization   Amrita Narliker

Since its inception, the World Trade Organization has generated debate, controversy, and even outrage. Its far-reaching impact on peoples' everyday lives makes the WTO a subject of importance not just to economists, but to everyone. It is simultaneously accused of both not doing enough and of doing too much, and its high-level meetings have come to be associated with impassioned and angry protests.

This book provides a timely exploration of what the WTO is, what it does, and the complicated politics involved in its negotiations and rulings. Confronting the controversy surrounding the WTO head-on, the author highlights issues of power, marginalization, and development, and raises the important question of whether it actually deserves the reputation it has come to acquire.

Machiavelli   **Quentin Skinner**

Machiavelli died nearly 500 years ago, but his name lives on as a byword for cunning, duplicity, and the exercise of bad faith in political affairs. Machiavelli's criticism of classical and contemporary humanism is a simple but devastating one. He argues that, if a ruler wishes to reach his highest goals, he will not always find it rational to be moral; on the contrary, he will find that any consistent attempt to cultivate the princely virtues will prove to be a ruinously irrational policy. But what of the Christian objection that this is a foolish as well as a wicked position to adopt, since it forgets the Day of Judgement on which all injustices will finally be punished? About this Machiavelli says nothing at all. His silence is eloquent, indeed epoch-making; it echoed around Christian Europe, at first eliciting a stunned silence in return, and then a howl of execration that has never finally died away.

> *'an informative study.'*   The Daily Telegraph

Gandhi   **Bhikhu Parekh**

Deeply unhappy with the basic thrust of modern civilization, Gandhi spent most of his adult life exploring an alternative. In Western thought such exploration has generally taken the form of constructing a Utopian, or ideal, society. Gandhi believed that, since different societies had different histories and traditions, the search for a single model was both incoherent and dangerous. For him, all that a critic could and should do was to suggest the general principles that should govern the good society, leaving each society free to realize them in its own unique way. Gandhi's regulative principles of the good society were derived from his theory of human nature. The good society should be informed by the spirit of cosmic piety. Since human beings are not masters or owners, but guardians, of the rest of creation, they should so organize their collective life that it respects the latter's integrity, diversity, rhythm, and inner balance, and make no greater demands on it than are required for a life of moderate comfort.

Economics   Partha Dasgupta

The Economist's Agenda

Economics in large measure tries to uncover the processes that influence how people's lives come to be what they are. The discipline also tries to identify ways to influence those very processes so as to improve the prospects of those who are hugely constrained in what they can be and do. The former activity involves finding explanations, while the latter tries to identify policy prescriptions. Economists also make forecasts of what the conditions of economic life are going to be; but if the predictions are to be taken seriously, they have to be built on an understanding of the processes that shape people's lives; which is why the attempt to explain takes precedence over forecasting.

The context in which explanations are sought or in which prescriptions are made could be a household, a village, a district, a country, or even the whole world – the extent to which people or places are aggregated merely reflects the details with which we choose to study the social world. Imagine that we wish to understand the basis on which food is shared among household members in a community. Household income would no doubt be expected to play a role; but we would need to look inside households if we are to discover whether food is allocated on the basis of age, gender, and status. If we find that it is, we should ask why they play a role and what policy prescriptions, if any, commend themselves. In contrast, suppose we want to know whether the world as a whole is wealthier today than it was fifty years ago. As the question is about global averages, we would be justified in ironing out differences within and among households.

Averaging is required over time as well. The purpose of the study and the cost of collecting information together influence the choice of the unit of time over which the averaging is done. Population census in India, for example, is conducted once every ten years. More frequent censuses would be far more costly and wouldn't yield information of any great importance. In contrast, if we are to study changes in the volume of home sales across seasons, even annual statistics would miss the point of the inquiry. Monthly statistics on home sales are a favourite compromise between detail and the cost of obtaining detail.

Forthcoming
African History, John Parker and Richard Rathbone
Antisemitism, Steven Beller
Citizenship, Richard Bellamy
Fundamentalism, Malise Ruthven
Human Migration, Khalid Koser
HIV/AIDS, Alan Whiteside
International Relations, Paul Wilkinson
Racism, Ali Rattansi

Chapter 5
Heaven and Hell

Introduction　　**by Damien Keown**

In today's 'global village' understanding one's own religion or culture is no longer enough: we need in addition to understand how and why our neighbour may see things differently. The series of Very Short Introductions includes many titles that illustrate how the enduring and deeply influential phenomenon of religious belief has influenced the major cultures and civilizations of the world.

The series includes volumes on Buddhism, Hinduism, Islam, and Judaism – with the recent volume on Christianity completing the set of five main world religions. There are further titles on some of the founders and significant historical figures of these religions, such as the Buddha and Saint Paul. Two Very Short Introductions introduce important religious scriptures – the Bible and the Koran – and another explores the broad subject of theology. This is a measure of the interest in the subject of religion in today's multicultural world.

Much of the most exciting contemporary work in theology and ethics is being produced at the interface of different religious traditions, where discussion generates insights and creative resolution of global problems. On issues such as human rights, poverty, the environment, and scientific developments in genetics, there is a surprising amount of convergence among religions. In the interfaith discussions I have attended, it has always seemed clear that there is much more that unites than divides the different religious traditions, an intuition that can be confirmed by browsing through the titles on religion in the VSI series.

But is it possible to condense such a vast topic as a religion – with its complex doctrines and often thousands of years of history – into a single volume, and a slim one at that? When asked to contribute to the series myself, I was sceptical that this could be done, but I am now a confirmed believer in the 'small is beautiful' approach to introductions. Requiring authors to focus only on the essentials produces a clearer and sharper picture. Once the key concepts have been grasped, longer supplementary works can be consulted as required, but the task of learning is greatly enhanced by a good primer.

Clearly, no short work can be exhaustive, but a surprising amount of information can be compressed into a small number of pages, especially by making skilful and appropriate use of text boxes, diagrams, maps, and chronologies, as the series manages to do. As an example, my own volume on Buddhism includes chapters discussing the nature and definition of Buddhism, the life of the Buddha, karma and cosmology, Buddhist doctrine, Mahayana Buddhism, Buddhist ethics, and Buddhism in the West. For the past few years I have used this volume as a set text for my undergraduate classes on Buddhism, with considerable success. Other authors in the series classify their subject in different ways, but each volume on the world religions provides the essential information required to understand the main teachings, beliefs, and historical evolution of that tradition and its place in the modern world.

It is precisely the challenges of modernity that will lead many readers, perplexed at contemporary events, to peruse these volumes in order to understand the motives of those who act in ways that otherwise seem incomprehensible. The tragic events of 11 September 2001 in New York, so graphically witnessed on television, continue to reverberate at a global level in social, political, and economic circles. Following these events, Americans have been reading introductory works on Islam at an unprecedented rate in an attempt to comprehend those who could strike at their country with such hatred. And it is not only Americans who are seeking to understand Islam – as the recent bombings in Bali and Kenya have demonstrated, Islamic fundamentalism is a global force that affects not just the United States. In this connection, the volume on Islam in this series, together with the forthcoming one on fundamentalism, will provide an excellent starting point for anyone seeking to comprehend the motives of groups like al-Qaida, and the relationship between political objectives, violence, and religious faith.

Many in the West, of course, have turned away from religion in favour of 'modernity', only to find the secular world, with its individualism and consumer values, spiritually unfulfilling. Writers such as Charles Taylor have described how the search for 'a momentary sense of wow!' has displaced religious life, leading to a feeling of drift, lack of practical conviction, and loss of meaning. Related to this is the phenomenon of religious consumerism – church and faith shopping – whereby religions are mixed and matched as required. Think of Madonna's mystical odyssey through Kabbalah, yoga, and Buddhism, or Bob Dylan's spiritual saga involving encounters with Christianity, Judaism, and atheism.

Although the phenomenon of declining church attendance is often adduced as an indicator of the progressive secularization of Western society (on average only some 20% of Europeans describe themselves as actively involved in religious practice), readers seem to have a greater appetite than ever for books about religion. In part this paradox may be explained by the fact that the 'West' is not a homogeneous entity: in a June 1998 CNN/USA Today Gallup poll, 62% of Americans said that religion is 'very important' in their own lives, 70% claimed to be members of a church or synagogue, and 40% said they had attended religious services the previous week.

One thing is for sure: religious pluralism is an essential feature of the modern world and is likely to remain so. The United States, apart from being the only remaining superpower, is now the most religiously diverse nation on earth. In a world where denominational loyalties are often entwined with racial, ethnic, or national identities, and where religious faith is often used (or misused) in the quest for political and military objectives, a sound understanding of the world's diverse faiths can go a long way to secure peace and harmony among nations.

Christianity   **Linda Woodhead**

Christianity has a vast reservoir of resources for shaping life and death. Like most religions it is more capacious and flexible than a philosophical system, and works not only with abstract concepts but with vivid stories, striking images, resonant symbols, and life-shaping rituals. It appeals to heart and senses as well as mind, and offers a range of prompts and provocations for guiding and shaping the lives of individuals and societies. There are nevertheless limits to what can count as Christian, for in opening up some possibilities for life and thought it rules out others.

At one end of the spectrum, we have forms of Christianity shaped by reverence for higher power. They focus on a God who infinitely transcends the world and human beings and rules over them. Such Christianity sees the good life – the holy life – as involving sacrifice of one's own (sinful) thoughts, choices, and desires in order to live up to the higher life that God requires. At the other end of the spectrum, we have something different: forms of Christianity that place less emphasis upon God's rule *over* human beings, and more emphasis upon the divine *in* the human. Rather than worship a God who remains high above human life, they focus upon the possibility of the divine coming into being in human life. As such, they place their emphasis not on power from above but power from below; not on power from outside but power from within. Interpretations of Jesus differ accordingly: for a Christianity of higher power, he is a transcendent being who must be obeyed;

whereas for a Christianity of inner power, he is a spiritual being who can inspire, in-Spirit, and divinize human life.

Anglicanism   Mark Chapman

With more than 70 million followers worldwide, Anglicanism is one of the most widespread expressions of Christianity. From its origins in the 16th century conflict with Rome, through its expansion with the British Empire, it has today diversified into a multitude of national churches across the globe.

Mark Chapman examines how Anglicanism is defined, and traces its history and development, along the way revealing what is distinctive about its theology. Highlighting the contemporary diversity of this worldwide phenomenon, Chapman also examines the problems it faces: from post-colonialism and secularisation to the headline-grabbing controversies over women priests and homosexuality. Chapman ends his account with thought-provoking suggestions of possible futures for the Anglican Communion.

Theology   David F. Ford

David Ford provides both believers and non-believers with a balanced survey of the central questions of contemporary theology. He inspects the principles underlying religious belief, including the centrality of salvation to most major religions, the changing concept of God over time, and the issue of sin and evil. He also probes the nature of experience, knowledge, and wisdom in theology, and discusses what is involved in interpreting theological texts today.

What about Jesus?

Considering Jesus theologically means neither taking the Jesus of mainstream Christian worship as the last word, nor being continually blown about by fashions. It is rather about pursuing, in ways that take seriously the best available scholarship and theological thinking, basic questions such as: How is the New Testament and other testimony to Jesus to be understood and assessed? What is to be made of the classic developments in Christian doctrine about Jesus, which lie behind the ways in which he is related to in contemporary Christian faith? What is the significance of the amazing variety of images and portrayals of Jesus through history and the world today?

'it succeeds brilliantly in its task of introduction.'

Stephen Sykes, Bishop of Ely

The Bible   John Riches

The Bible is one of the most influential and widely read books in the world, selling 2.5 billion copies between 1815 and 1975, and translated into over 350 different languages. Here, the author looks at the importance accorded to the Bible by different communities and cultures and attempts to explain why it has generated such a rich variety of uses and interpretations.

Rogue editions of the Bible

Printers' errors and unusual translations have led to a number of versions of the Bible gaining nicknames. These are some of the better known:

Printers' Bible: with 'Printers' for 'Princes' in Psalm 119:161, producing, for the publishers, the finely appropriate sentence: 'Printers have persecuted me without a cause.'

Vinegar Bible: 1717 edition with a running title for Luke 22 reading 'the parable of the vinegar', for 'vineyard'.

Wicked Bible: 1632 edition in which the seventh commandment reads: 'Thou shalt commit adultery.'

'offers a balanced, scholarly overview.'   The Independent

The Dead Sea Scrolls   Timothy H. Lim

If media attention and sales figures are anything to go by, there is no doubt that the most sensational aspects of research are related to the link between the scrolls and the origins of the Early Church. As mentioned in the opening chapter, even a whiff of controversy, especially involving the Vatican, will send journalists scurrying to investigate. The appetite of the public for plots involving the Dead Sea Scrolls remains unabated; secrecy, back-room deals, and spin-doctoring appeal to the human psyche that seeks to glimpse into a covert world of political and religious machinations beneath the ordered and institutionalized edifice of established religion.

The Koran   Michael Cook

The Koran has constituted a remarkably resilient core of identity and continuity for a religious tradition that is now in its 50th century. Today, there are significant Muslim populations of diverse ethnic origins in all major Western countries. The total number of Muslims in the world is somewhat over a billion, comprising almost one-fifth of the world's population. To help the reader understand this important religion, Michael Cook provides a lucid and direct account of the significance of the Koran both in the modern world and in that of traditional Islam.

Each of the major Eurasian traditions that dominate the history of literate culture has possessed some body of authoritative texts, the transmission of which has been central to its continuing identity. The Greeks had their Homer, the Jews and Christians their Bible, the Zoroastrians their Avesta, the Hindus their Vedas, and the Muslims their Koran. In terms of character and content, these texts do not have much in common. What they share is their centrality to their respective cultures.

'informative, witty, and rich with insight. The author firmly

Islam   **Malise Ruthven**

The purpose of Islam

The word Islam means in Arabic 'self-surrender'; it is closely related etymologically to *salaam*, the word for peace. The universal greeting with which Muslims address one other, and foreigners, is *as salaam 'alaikum* – peace be upon you.

If there is a single word that can be taken to represent the primary impulse of Islam, be it theological, political, or sociological, it is *tawhid* – making one, unicity. Although the word does not occur in the Koran, the concept it articulates is implicit in the credal formula *there is no god but God*, and there are references to the God who is without partners or associates throughout the holy text. The absolute insistence that it is unicity above all that defines divinity appears in striking, if ironic, contrast with the disunity observable in the Muslim world. It is as if the aspiration to realize divine unicity in terms of the social and political order is forever destined to wreck itself on the shores of human perversity.

Judaism   **Norman Solomon**

Discussing Judaism as a living religion, in all its contemporary richness and variety, the author provides a perceptive and often humorous introduction to the central features and characters of Judaism, from its spiritual leaders, poets, and philosophers, to its eccentrics, including the mystic who tried to convert the pope and the Berber princess who held up the Arab invasion of Spain. The emphasis lies with the *creative* history of Judaism. The suffering and the persecutions and the forced migrations cannot be denied, but amazingly throughout the centuries the spirit has flourished with a still unending procession of poets and saints, of philosophers and of Bible commentators, of grammarians and talmudists, of lawyers and satirists and pastors, of unsung women and men of humble faith.

> *'Norman Solomon has achieved the near impossible with his enlightened book . . . a small masterpiece.'*
>
> Rabbi Julia Neuberger

Buddhism   **Damien Keown**

From its origins in India over 2,000 years ago, Buddhism has spread throughout Asia and is now exerting an increasing influence on Western culture. In clear and straightforward language, the author explains how Buddhism began and how it evolved into its present-day form.

What does Buddhism tell us?

Everything

In a very real sense individuals create themselves through their moral choices. By freely and repeatedly choosing certain things, an individual shapes his character, and through his character his future. As the proverb has it: 'Sow an act, reap a habit; sow a habit, reap a character; sow a character, reap a destiny.'

It is desire, in the form of a strong addiction to life and the pleasant experiences that it offers, that causes rebirth. If the five factors of individuality (the physical body, sensations and feelings, cognition, character traits and dispositions, and consciousness or sentiency) are likened to a car, then desire is the fuel that propels it forward.

> *'impressive'*
>
> Irish Times

Buddha   **Michael Carrithers**

The author guides us through the diverse accounts of the life and teaching of the Buddha. He discusses the social and political background of India in the Buddha's time, and traces the development of his thought. Though the Buddha witnessed his world comprehensively, he was not of it. He was set apart by the high-minded personal morality of the renouncers: 'as a lotus flower is born in water, grows in water, and rises out of water to stand above it unsoiled, so I, born in the world, raised in the world, having overcome the world, live unsoiled by the world'.

'a readable and wonderfully lucid introduction to one of mankind's most beautiful, profound, and compelling systems of wisdom. His impressive powers of explanation help us to come to terms with a vital contemporary reality.'

Bryan Appleyard

Buddhist Ethics   **Damien Keown**

Karma

The doctrine of karma is concerned with the ethical implications of Dharma, in particular those relating to the consequences of moral behaviour. Kharma is not a system of rewards and punishments meted out by God but a kind of natural law akin to the law of gravity. In popular usage in the West, karma is thought of simply as the good and bad things that happen to a person, a little like good and bad luck. However, this oversimplifies what for Buddhists is a complex of interrelated ideas which embraces both ethics and belief in reincarnation. The literal meaning of the Sanskrit word karma is 'action', but karma as a religious concept is concerned not with just any actions but with actions of a particular kind. Karmic actions are moral actions, and the Buddha defined karma by reference to moral choices and the acts consequent upon them. He stated, 'It is intention (*cetanā*), O monks, that I call karma; having willed one acts through body, speech, or mind' (A.iii.415).

Hinduism   **Kim Knott**

In what forms does Hinduism appear in contemporary life?

Hindu gods and goddesses are everywhere in India, hidden within gorgeous temples and small wayside shrines, depicted in intricate stone carvings, looking out benevolently from advertisements. They are featured on calendar prints and film posters, and captured on market stalls and in shop windows, in jewellery and small scriptures. They are woven into the fabric of life in Indian villages and cities, and are now also to be found in Hindu communities from the Caribbean to North America and the UK, from South Africa to Thailand.

'Miracle', 'hallucination', 'simple scientific explanation', 'divine grace', or 'politically inspired hoax' ran the headlines as onlookers sought to explain why, on 22 September 1995, images of Ganesha the world over were devouring the milk offered to them by their devout followers. The old debate between science and faith was rekindled. Hindus themselves were quietly divided over the phenomenon, but their surprise was not so much at its occurrence as at its scale. Divine manifestations and small miracles are believed to be commonplace in Indian religious life, but that Hindus and their non-Hindu friends around the globe should witness Ganesha's gracious act was extraordinary.

> *'instantly accessible without being in any way condescending or an oversimplification . . . issues conveyed with an elegance and simplicity'*
>
> Julia Leslie, SOAS, London

Sikhism   **Eleanor Nesbitt**

Sikhism is often portrayed as a neat package consisting of a founder (Guru Nanak), a scripture (the Guru Granth Sahib), places of worship known as gurdwaras, and the requirement to show one's allegiance physically (by not cutting one's hair, for example). In what follows, at every stage of the Sikh story, the not so neat processes involved in emerging as a distinct religion will be evident. These include Sikhs' continually evolving sense of identity, often in relation to their Hindu neighbours. These processes are still underway and spark passionate debate.

People who identify themselves as Sikhs answer the question 'Who is a Sikh?' in different ways. One authoritative definition is:

> any human being who faithfully believes in:
>
> One immortal Being
> Ten Gurus, from Guru Nanak to Guru Gobind Singh
> The Guru Granth Sahib
> The utterances and teachings of the ten Gurus and
> The baptism bequeathed by the tenth Guru
> and who does not owe allegiance to any other religion.

Paul   E. P. Sanders

Paul is the most powerful human personality in the history of the Church. A missionary, theologian, and religious genius, he laid down in his epistles the foundations on which later Christian theology was built. In this highly original introduction to Paul's life and thought, the author pays equal attention to Paul's fundamental convictions and the sometimes convoluted ways in which they worked out.

Why is Paul so important to us today?

He forces us, in fact, to pose an extremely serious question: must a religion, in addressing diverse problems, offer answers that are completely consistent with one another? Is it not good to have passionate hopes and commitments that cannot all be reduced to a scheme in which they are arranged in a hierarchical relationship?

> *'Sanders makes one think afresh about all sorts of issues . . . read this book.'*
>
> Hebrew Christian

Atheism   Julian Baggini

The author provides a positive case for atheism, one which is not simply about rubbishing religious belief, and writes as much about why one should be an atheist as why one should *not* be an atheist.

We human beings often claim that it is our ability to think that distinguishes us from other animals. We are *homo sapiens* – thinking hominids – and our capacity to reason is our distinctive and highest feature. Yet we are not purely rational. It is not just that we are often in the grip of irrational or non-rational forces and desires, it is that our thinking is itself infused with emotion. These feelings shape our thought, often without us realizing it. This book puts forward the rational case for atheism. If we are to make the case for any point of view, the best way to do so is always to appeal to reasons and arguments that can command the widest possible support. Unfortunately, we often approach rational discussions with prejudices, fears, and commitments. Some of these are not founded on reason and that confers on them a certain immunity to the powers of rational argumentation. So it is with atheism, about which few readers will have a neutral outlook.

Chapter 6
Expressing ourselves

Introduction   **Catherine Belsey**

Some people see the arts – painting and sculpture, literature, music, and architecture – as an extra, society's pleasurable reward for carrying out the serious work of science and technology, or manufacturing and sales, come to that. From this point of view, culture gratifies the senses, while science addresses the intellect. But these same people might also concede that the pictures we like, the buildings we feel happy in, and the fiction we choose may tell us something about who we are. Tastes differ, and the differences can be revealing.

The visual arts thrive on controversy these days. Ever since Marcel Duchamp offered a readymade urinal for exhibition in 1917 under the title *Fountain*, artists have apparently vied with each other to outrage the public. Gratifying the senses seems to have gone by the board. Instead, the project looks more like a challenge to the viewer. 'Is it art?', these works seem to ask; 'what is art?'; 'what do we *mean* by art?' In that sense, art poses an intellectual question to the spectator as an individual, and at the same time to society in general. As Cynthia Freeland makes clear in her *Art Theory: A Very Short Introduction*, art has become a conceptual issue, as well as – or instead of? – a pleasure, according to preference.

Tastes vary, and the variations are not always arbitrary or accidental. Monticello, for instance, the house built in the 1770s by Thomas Jefferson, a prominent founder of the American constitution, is elegant, classical, and restrained. It owes its dignity to a direct line of descent from the temples of ancient Greece and Rome, and in the eyes of an observer familiar, however unconsciously, with the authority of this tradition in Western culture, Monticello justifies its understated claim to power. But as Andrew Ballantyne points out in his *Architecture: A Very Short Introduction*, if my ancestors were first-nation Americans who lived on this land without claiming to own it, I might be considerably less impressed by the 'civilized' values of the classical tradition. And if I were descended from the slaves who worked the Monticello plantation, I might well see the same building as symbolizing oppression.

If cultural difference affects our tastes and preferences, does it also play a part in defining who we are? Debates about the influence of violence on television remain unresolved, but most people would probably agree that the characteristics cultures attribute to fictional heroes and villains can tell us a good deal about the values of society. What do 'we' value in our increasingly globalized culture? Courage, evidently, and intelligence, though not necessarily the academic kind. Our fictional detectives and doctors possess an intuitive knowledge and a skill that cannot be taught. Masculinity and

8. The Parthenon, Athens, Greece (447–436 BC)

femininity matter, though mercifully that antithesis is gradually becoming less sharply demarcated.

Did the Greeks value the same qualities? On the evidence of their myths and epics, they rated independence; wisdom, to a high degree; and possibly voracious bisexual appetites. And the Romans? Military skill, stoicism, and voracious heterosexual appetites. The difference of other cultures throws into relief the specificity of the values we so easily take for granted in our own.

What makes us the people we are? Since the late 1800s it has come increasingly to seem that we are as much the products of culture as its origin. Most recently poststructuralist theory, in particular, has argued that the ways we think and feel are defined by the meanings we learn. From birth, we are surrounded by a mother tongue that is already in place. Small children learn – and learn to reproduce – the meanings and values inscribed in the language that constitutes their culture. Fortunately, this doesn't make us into robots. We learn a number of cultural dialects – one for the classroom and another for the playground, say – and these jostle for control, or propel us in unexpected directions. But it might help to explain the 'obviousness' of certain values.

In my *Poststructuralism: A Very Short Introduction* I put the case that, because we learn so early that 'democracy', say, is positive and 'dictatorship' wrong, and because many of us learn this before we know much about the details of the political practices the words define, it can seem to go without saying that it would be worth going to war to defend our 'democratic' way of life. Our antagonist, however, might take for granted a quite different set of meanings and values, in which religion was more important than political systems, or revealed truth mattered more than voting. And if poststructuralist theory is right, these values go deep.

No one in their right mind would claim that cultural differences alone cause wars, would they? Probably not: the material and economic issues are at least as important. But if cultures play a significant part in global conflict, cultural issues matter, and the study of culture, and cultures, might be as important as an understanding of science and technology. Some people would even say our survival could depend on it.

Would they have a point? Current theories about culture and the arts are nothing if not controversial. What do *you* think?

Myth   Robert Segal

There is no one version of any myth. There are perhaps as many versions of a story as tellings of that story. Theories of myth go back to ancient times. Plato and the Stoics are the best-known ancient theorists, and they offer contrary approaches to myth. Modern theories hail from long-standing disciplines such as philosophy, religious studies, and literature, but modern theories come most effusively from the social sciences – anthropology, sociology, and psychology. Most disciplines harbour multiple theories. To study myth is to apply to it one or more theories from one or more disciplines.

Literary Theory   Jonathan Culler

What is literature? If a five-year-old is asking, it's easy. 'Literature', you answer, 'is stories, poems, plays.' But if the questioner is a literary theorist, it's harder to know how to take the query. 'What is literature?' asks not for a definition but for an analysis, even an argument, about why one might concern oneself with literature at all.

How can we define literature?

Are there any essential, distinguishing features that literary works share? Works of literature come in all shapes and sizes, and most of

Anthony Haden-Guest

9. 'You're a terrorist? Thank God. I understood Meg to say you were a theorist.'

them seem to have more in common with works that aren't usually called literature than with some other works recognized as literature. Charlotte Brontë's *Jane Eyre*, for instance, more closely resembles an autobiography than it does a sonnet, and a poem by Robert Burns – 'My love is like a red, red rose' – resembles a folk-song more than it does Shakespeare's *Hamlet*. Are there qualities shared by poems, plays, and novels that distinguish them from, say, songs, transcripts of conversations, and autobiographies?

'It is impossible to imagine a clearer treatment of the subject, or one that is, within the given limits of length, more comprehensive.'

Sir Frank Kermode

Postmodernism   Christopher Butler

Christopher Butler considers postmodernist artists, intellectual gurus, academic critics, philosophers, and social scientists as if they were all members of a loosely constituted and quarrelsome political party. This party is by and large internationalist and 'progressive'. It is on the left rather than the right, and it tends to see everything, from abstract painting to personal relationships, as political undertakings. It is not particularly unified in doctrine, and even those who have most significantly contributed ideas to its manifestos sometimes indignantly deny membership – and yet the postmodernist party tends to believe that its time has come. It is certain of its uncertainty, and often claims that it has seen through the sustaining illusions of others, and so has grasped the 'real' nature of the cultural and political institutions which surround us. In doing this postmodernists often follow Marx. They claim to be peculiarly aware of the unique state of contemporary society, immured as it is in what they call 'the postmodern condition'.

The new ideas represented by postmodernism, although they came to inspire some literature, and to dominate its interpretation in academic circles, were actually rooted outside the arts. Of the movement's protagonists, for example, Barthes was mainly interested in the application of linguistic models to the interpretation of text, Derrida's philosophical work began as a critique of linguistics, and Foucault's base was in the social sciences and history. They were also all guided to a greater or lesser degree by the re-reading or redemption of Marx.

> 'a pre-eminently sane, lucid, and concise statement about the central issues, the key examples, and the notorious derelictions of postmodernism.'
>
> Ihab Hassan, University of Wisconsin, Milwaukee

Barthes   Jonathan Culler

Barthes is famous for contradictory reasons. To many, he is above all a theorist, a structuralist, perhaps *the* structuralist, advocate of a systematic, scientific approach to cultural phenomena. To others, Barthes stands for the pleasures of reading and the reader's right to read idiosyncratically. Against a literary criticism focused on authors – interested in recovering what authors thought or meant – Barthes champions the reader and promotes literature that gives the reader an active, creative role.

The theorist as author

Yet this enemy of authors is himself pre-eminently an author, a writer whose varied products reveal a personal style and vision. Many of Barthes' works are idiosyncratic, falling outside established genres: *L'Empire des signes* combines touristic commentary on Japan with a reflection on signs in everyday life and their ethical implications; and *Roland Barthes par Roland Barthes* is a strangely detached account of the life and works of one 'Roland Barthes' that evades the conventions of autobiography.

Poststructuralism   Catherine Belsey

Poststructuralism proposes that the distinctions we make are not necessarily given by the world around us, but are instead produced by the symbolizing systems we learn. How else would we know the difference between pixies and gnomes? But we learn our native tongue at such an early age that it seems transparent, a window on to a world of things, even if some of those things are in practice imaginary, no more than ideas of things, derived from children's stories. Poststructuralists don't (normally) doubt that there is a world: their anxiety concerns what we can claim to know about it with any certainty.

> *'A wonderfully clear account.'* The Guardian

Postcolonialism   Robert J. Young

Postcolonialism describes both an historical condition and a transformation of ways of thinking about the world. Although some former colonies have been 'postcolonial' since the 18th century, 'postcolonialism' is the product of the 20th-century independence movements and the subsequent decolonization of the former empires of Britain, France, Belgium, Holland, Portugal, and the USSR, from 1947 to 1997. Postcolonialism names the political, social, and cultural effects of these historical processes. It also continues the challenge to Western dominance and Western formations of knowledge that constituted the basis of the anti-colonial movements. Although the power relations between empire and colony, centre and margin, have often been reinforced economically since independence, at the same time the identity of 'the West' itself has been subverted through migration, diaspora, and cultural transformation. The politics of postcolonialism began with the deconstruction of ethnocentric assumptions in Western knowledge.

Linguistics   Peter Matthews

What would an outsider make of the noises *Homo sapiens* so volubly produces? The words people use are never fixed for all time. *Grotty*, for example, was a new word when it was coined in Britain in the 1960s, and the usage of many speakers of English who were alive at that time has changed to include it. *Gay* in the sense of 'homosexual' seems to have had its origin in prison slang, and in 1950s Britain could still be explained, in a passage cited in *The Oxford English Dictionary*, as 'an American Euphemism'. It has since become familiar, however, even in the speech of many older people who, when they were young, had known it mainly in such phrases as *gay bachelor* or as Wordsworth used it ('A poet cannot but be gay') in his poem about daffodils.

> *'full of facts and figures . . . Matthews has carried off a difficult job with real panache. I would recommend this very warmly indeed.'*
>
> Andrew Linn, University of Sheffield

Cryptography   **Fred Piper and Sean Murphy**

In this fascinating introduction to how cryptography actually works, the authors highlight its all-pervasive impact on modern society. In doing so, they demystify the art of cryptography, highlighting the difficulties and ever-increasing importance of data protection and authentication in the modern world.

Cryptography has been a significant historical influence for more than 2,000 years. Traditionally its main users were governments and the military. Prior to the 1970s, cryptography was a 'black art', understood and practised by only a few government and military personnel. It is now a well-established academic discipline that is taught in many universities.

> *'A perfect pocket primer for anyone interested in Cryptography.'*
>
> Simon Singh

Shakespeare   **Germaine Greer**

The chief pitfall threatening any discussion of Shakespeare's thought is the common assumption that the opinions of any character in a Shakespearian play are Shakespeare's own. Shakespeare was not a propagandist; he did not write plays as vehicles for his own ideas. Rather he developed a theatre of dialectical conflict, in which idea is pitted against idea and from their friction a deeper understanding of the issues emerges. The resolution which is reached is not the negation of the conflict, but the stasis produced by art. Even as we applaud it, we recognize its fragility. It might be said that the strength of Shakespeare's position is that he refrains from coming to conclusions but leaves that to those who complete his utterance, the audience and the actors in the theatre.

Characters and identity

Shakespeare's characters are not defined by their actions, nor are their personalities rigid constructs which control their capacity for action. His personages search for ways to transcend that identity, which is transitory, and free the spirit, which is made in God's likeness, eternal and immutable.

> *'the clearest and simplest explanation of Shakespeare's thought I have yet read'*
>
> Auberon Waugh

Tragedy   **Adrian Poole**

Open the paper, turn on the news, and sooner or later you'll meet the words 'tragic' and 'tragedy'. Even as I write, 19 Chinese cockle-pickers are reported drowned in Morecambe Bay, Lancashire. 'The gangs behind the tragedy are on the run', one headline assures us. The story attracts no fewer than ten more 'tragedies' across two reports and a leader in the *Guardian* (7 February 2004). Tragedy: how many more times, of how many more disasters, before you read *this*? Even as this goes to press, the number of lives lost to the Asian tsunami and its aftermath appears literally countless.

It's easy to feel overwhelmed by the word. Once it meant something special, as it did to John Milton, writing in the middle of the 17th century:

Sometime let gorgeous Tragedy
In sceptred pall come sweeping by,
Presenting Thebes, or Pelops' line,
Or the tale of Troy divine.
Or what (though rare) of later age,
Ennobled hath the buskined stage.

He is thinking of Tragedy as a regal figure from ancient Greece, like Oedipus (from Thebes) and Agamemnon (descendant of Pelops) and the heroes from Homer's *Iliad* (the tale of Troy), and he dresses them up with lofty old words like 'pall' (robe) and 'buskin' (the high thick-soled boot supposedly worn by the actors in Athenian tragedy). It's a long way from the tale of those Chinese cockle-pickers. Nothing gorgeous about *them*. No sceptred palls or buskins in evidence, no connection with ancient myth, and not much chance of dramatic ennobling. For Milton, tragedy was not something that happens every day. It was an idea attached to a specific form of drama performed at special times and places, at the religious festivals of ancient Athens and the courts of modern kings and noblemen.

Kafka   **Ritchie Robertson**

'When Gregor Samsa awoke one morning from troubled dreams he found himself transformed in his bed into a monstrous insect.' This must be Kafka's most famous sentence. But, like many Kafka sentences, it is full of puzzles. Gregor's body is transformed, but his mind remains human: is 'himself' synonymous with his body, as opposed to his mind? And Gregor does not exactly 'find' himself transformed: rather, although he sees his brown belly and numerous legs, he fails to register this incomprehensible fact. After briefly wondering 'What has happened to me?', he reverts to the consciousness of a busy commercial traveller who has to get up early on a wet morning to catch the 5 o'clock train.

Gregor's transformation into an insect drastically expresses Kafka's ambivalence towards his body and towards the body in general. His transformation and his failure to notice it convey the degree to which Gregor is alienated from his own body. He has to cope with the concrete task of getting a large and unwieldy insect body out of bed, still believing that he must and will catch his train. His obsession with his job reveals the self-estrangement imposed on him by its demands. 'That boy thinks of nothing but his work,' his mother assures the chief clerk of Gregor's firm, who, exercising an implausibly but alarmingly thorough surveillance, has come to see why he wasn't at the station. Even so, mind and body are linked by the language of the unconscious, which can involuntarily reveal the truth. Still lying in bed, Gregor reflects that one of his colleagues is 'a mere creature [*Kreatur*] of the chief, spineless and stupid'. The word 'spineless' betrays Gregor's unconscious awareness that he himself is now an invertebrate. This commerce between the body and the unconscious mind blurs the contrast between Gregor's human mind and animal body.

The Marquis de Sade   **John Phillips**

Sade wrote an impressive amount during his 74 years. However, much of it has not survived. A number of manuscripts were confiscated and destroyed by the authorities during his time at Charenton, while others were burned after his death at the family's behest. Among the works that have endured until the present day are many conventionally written plays, stories, and verses, but Sade's sulphurous reputation rests upon those three obscene works that were already in the public domain in the 1790s (*Justine*, *Philosophy in the Boudoir*, and *Juliette*), together with *The 120 Days of Sodom*, the loss of which in the Revolution ironically preserved the work for posterity.

Russian Literature   **Catriona Kelly**

The uniqueness of Russian literature (and Russian culture more generally) has been held by many Western observers to lie in precisely its ability to embrace spiritual and material worlds. *Judging* life has been a constant preoccupation of Russian writers, while Pushkin himself is an illustration that intelligent Russians have had just as large a talent for, and inclination towards, *analysis* as their counterparts anywhere in the world. In Russia itself, writers have often been regarded as sages, as moral guides to how life should be lived; but there are many other reasons for reading Russian literature. Like any other literature, it represents the world in new and extraordinary ways, it investigates areas of human experience that we sometimes prefer not to think about (madness, homicidal urges, tyranny); and it offers not only intellectual stimulation but the sensual delight of language stretched to its limits, of laughter, and of flights of imaginative fancy.

> *'brilliant ... , written with elegance, ... informed, incisive, provocative'*
>
> Anthony Cross, University of Cambridge

Art History   **Dana Arnold**

> A thing of beauty is a joy forever
>
> Keats

Can art have a history? We think about art as being timeless, the 'beauty' of its appearance having meaning, significance, and appeal to humankind across the ages. At least this usually applies to our ideas about 'high', or fine, art, in other words painting and sculpture. This kind of visual material can have an autonomous existence – we can enjoy looking at it for its own sake, independent of any knowledge of its context, although of course viewers from different time periods or cultures may see the same object in contrasting ways.

For art to have a history we expect not only a timeless quality but also some kind of sequence or progression, as this is what history leads us to expect. Our history books are full of events in the past that are presented as part of either the continual movement towards improvement, or as stories about great men, or as epochs of time that stand out from others – for instance, the Italian Renaissance or the Enlightenment. In regard to these kinds of frameworks for thinking about the past, the history of art does not disappoint. In the coming together of these two separate strands, we see how history reorders visual experience, making it take a range of forms. The most popular of these include writing about the history of art from the point of view of artists – usually 'great men'. Alternatively, we find art historians have sought to define the great stylistic epochs in the history of art, for example the Renaissance, Baroque, or Post-Impressionism. Each of these traditions can be written about independently of the others and they have provided a backbone for histories of art.

Art Theory   **Cynthia Freeland**

During a lecture by the prominent environmental artist Robert Irwin, he commented a bit cynically about the vagueness of the term 'art' that it 'has come to mean so many things that it doesn't mean anything any more'. But this didn't stop Irwin from offering his own definition. He proposed to describe art as 'a continuous examination of our perceptual awareness and a continuous expansion of our awareness of the world around us'. This challenging analysis of many centuries of art considers the question: What is art?

Message and meaning

Gender and sexual preference – together with nationality, ethnicity, politics, and religion – all seem to have some impact on the meaning of art. People have debated for centuries about the meaning of some works of art – for example, the *Mona Lisa*'s smile.

Does art bear a message in the way language does? What must we know to clarify an artwork's meaning: external facts about artists' lives, or internal facts about how their works were made? Can't we just look at an artwork for enjoyment?

'admirable for its scope, compactness and exceptional clarity. Reader-friendly and thought-provoking'

The Independent

Christian Art   **Beth Williamson**

The view that images were helpful to those whose levels of literacy were not high enough to read the Latin scriptures unaided became a widespread justification for the decoration of church buildings with images, and Christian writers from the time of Gregory onwards reiterated this opinion. For example, the Venerable Bede, the 8th-century monk of the monastery of Wearmouth-Jarrow in the North of England, defended depictions of sacred stories for instructive as well as ornamental purposes, so that 'those who are not capable of reading words may learn the works of our Lord and Saviour by looking at these images'. However, in another sermon, Bede introduced a slightly different understanding of the effect of religious imagery when he remarked that pictures could 'recall to the memory of the faithful' events such as the Crucifixion, or other Christian miracles. This is an important distinction, as Bede appears to argue here that pictures can remind viewers of that which they already know, rather than teach them what they do not know, and what they cannot read in scripture. In other words, Bede's understanding of religious imagery here (and that of several other later writers) is that such pictures fulfil a recollective rather than an instructive function.

Renaissance Art   **Geraldine A. Johnson**

Renaissance art, whether sacred, secular, or somewhere in between, was full of stories. Indeed, one of the primary functions of art in general in this period was to communicate stories and ideas by visual means to contemporary beholders in ways that were often more enticing, vivid, and memorable than was possible in a text, sermon, or speech alone. As Alberti put it in the 1430s, the most successful visual narrative, or *istoria*, was one that was 'so agreeably and pleasantly attractive that it will capture the eye of whatever learned or unlearned person is looking at it and will move his soul'. In the public realm, narrative altarpieces (both painted and sculpted in three dimensions), predella panels depicting saints' lives, paintings for confraternities, grand fresco cycles in churches, and classically inspired palace decorations not only helped beholders remember particular stories through their attractive imagery, but also inevitably reflected the personal, political, and social agendas of the people or organizations that had commissioned them. Sometimes, as in the case of illuminated manuscripts or a set of narrative prints, story-telling could be a more private, even intimate, activity involving just one person holding a book or sheet of paper in his or her hands. But even in such instances, how a particular story was told pictorially, and how it was interpreted, depended very much on the interests, beliefs, and priorities of the patron and his or her contemporary beholders.

Modern Art   **David Cottington**

Among the most visible developments in the reception of modern art has been the extraordinary growth in recent years in the numbers of people visiting 'blockbuster' exhibitions of what we could call 'blue-chip' modernism, in particular retrospectives of the work of major modernist painters. Exhibitions of Cézanne, Matisse, Picasso, and even – given the austerity and apparent emptiness of his abstract paintings – Rothko in the capital cities of the West in the past decade have drawn unprecedented numbers of viewers, and required previously-unheard-of crowd management strategies of advance booking and timed entry. Is this an expression of a nostalgia for the relative certainties of meaning (and of aesthetic reward) obtainable from painting, even modern abstract painting, in the face of the free-for-all that is contemporary art? If so, then it would mean that the rough-edged iconoclasm and outrageous inventiveness for which modernist artists were both celebrated and condemned not so long ago have been worn down surprisingly quickly, softened into accustomed cultural 'furniture' – ironically, to function rather like the 'armchair for a tired businessman' that Matisse in 1908 hoped, optimistically, that his painting would be seen as. This may be part of the reason. For Picasso was the key figure for modern art through most of the 20th century, and the vigour and outrageous inventiveness of his imagination were both a model for modernist art-makers and a target for their opponents; but the ascendancy of conceptual art in the 1970s and thereafter was secured on the shoulders of Marcel Duchamp – and so unforgivingly, obscurely intellectual was the new model of art-making that *he* offered, that the visual complexities of post-Picasso painting have perhaps seemed sheer hedonism in comparison.

Contemporary Art   Julian Stallabrass

It is a basic art-world orthodoxy, echoed just about everywhere, that contemporary art is ungraspably complex and diverse. The variety of contemporary forms, techniques, and subject-matter in art is indeed bewildering. The conventional media of painting, sculpture, and print-making have been overlaid with installation and 'new media', which can encompass anything from online art to computer-controlled sound environments. Artists cultivate for themselves images that range from traditional guru or shaman roles to beady-eyed, tongue-in-cheek chancer and careerist, and personas that include starstruck adolescent girls and engorged, axe-wielding psychotics. Art's concerns are also various, touching upon feminism, identity politics, mass culture, shopping, and trauma. Perhaps art's fundamental condition is to be unknowable (that concepts embodied in visual form can encompass contradiction), or perhaps those that hold to this view are helping to conceal a different uniformity.

Dada and Surrealism   **David Hopkins**

The 'avant-garde'

More than anything else, Dada and Surrealism were 'avant-garde' movements. The term 'avant-garde', which was first employed by the French utopian socialist Henri de Saint-Simon in the 1820s, initially had military connotations, but came to signify the advanced socio-political as well as aesthetic position to which the modern artist should aspire. Broadly speaking, art in the 19th century was synonymous with bourgeois individualism. Owned by the bourgeoisie or shown in bourgeois institutions, it was a means by which members of that class could temporarily escape the material constraints and contradictions of everyday existence. This state of affairs was challenged in the 1850s by the Realism of the French painter Gustave Courbet, which, by fusing a socialist agenda with a matching aesthetic credo, arguably represents the first self-consciously avant-garde tendency in art. By the early 20th century, several key art movements – such as Futurism in Italy, Constructivism in Russia, or De Stijl in Holland, as well as Dada and Surrealism – were pledged to contesting any separation between art and the contingent experience of the modern world.

Architecture   **Andrew Ballantyne**

We are shaped by the culture that we grow up in, and by the culture in which we participate, whether we think about it or not – and most of the time we don't think about it at all. In architecture, as in any other culture, our sense of 'how things should be' develops from our experience. Each gesture we make means something, but the meaning depends on the culture in which the gesture is understood.

Our experience of architecture

The precise ways in which we respond to buildings vary according to our prior experiences of buildings. Cutting across all considerations of style and taste, we respond also to the kind of life that we suppose to be implied in a building – whether it feels wholesome or dispiriting, sordid or dangerous, whether it opens up new possibilities, or reminds us of places where we have been happy in the past. This is an introduction not just to the way buildings are designed and made, but the way in which we live with them and confer meaning upon them.

> *'a densely fascinating guide'*
>
> The Guardian

Music   **Nicholas Cook**

It's an obvious fact that the world is teeming with different kinds of music: traditional, folk, classical, jazz, rock, pop, world, just to name a few. This has always been the case, but modern communications and sound reproduction technology have made musical pluralism part of everyday life. And yet the ways we think about music don't reflect this. Each type of music comes with its own way of thinking about music, as if it were the *only* way of thinking about music (and the only music to think about). In particular, the way of thinking about music that is built into schools and universities – and most books about music, for that matter – reflects the way music was in 19th-century Europe rather than the way it is today, anywhere. The result is a kind of credibility gap between music and how we think about it. In today's world, deciding what music to listen to is a significant part of deciding and announcing to people not just who you want to be . . . but who you *are*.

> *'a lively and lucid book . . . as a brief guide to the contemporary rethinking of music, it could hardly be bettered.'*
>
> BBC Music

World Music   **Philip Bohlman**

At the beginning of the 21st century it is impossible to define world music without slipping down a tautological slope. World music can be folk music, art music, or popular music; its practitioners may be amateur or professional. World music may be sacred, secular, or commercial; its performers may emphasize authenticity, while at the same time relying heavily on mediation to disseminate it to as many markets as possible. There's ample justification to call just about anything world music. Local musicians become dependent on the global music industry. Traditional melody and functions must undergo transformation in order to be mapped on Western harmony and repackaged for global consumption.

> *'Philip Bohlman's superb study places world music squarely in history – and a lengthy history at that, reaching back to the Age of Discovery and even beyond.'*
>> Richard Middleton, University of Newcastle upon Tyne

Design   **John Heskett**

So how can design be understood in a meaningful, holistic sense? Beyond all the confusion created by the froth and bubble of advertising and publicity, beyond the visual pyrotechnics of virtuoso designers seeking stardom, beyond the pronouncements of design gurus and the snake-oil salesmen of lifestyles, lies a simple truth. Design is one of the basic characteristics of what it is to be human, and an essential determinant of the quality of human life. It affects everyone in every detail of every aspect of what they do throughout each day. As such, it matters profoundly. Very few aspects of the material environment are incapable of improvement in some significant way by greater attention being paid to their design. Inadequate lighting, machines that are not user-friendly, badly formatted information, are just a few examples of bad design that create cumulative problems and tensions. It is therefore worth asking: if these things are a necessary part of our existence, why are they often done so badly? There is no simple answer. Cost factors are sometimes advanced in justification, but the margin between doing something well or badly can be exceedingly small, and cost factors can in fact be reduced by appropriate design inputs. The use of the term 'appropriate', however, is an important qualification.

The spectrum of capabilities covered by the term 'design' requires that means be carefully adapted to ends. A solution to a practical problem which ignores all aspects of its use can be disastrous, as would, say, medical equipment if it were treated as a vehicle for individual expression of fashionable imagery.

Journalism   Ian Hargreaves

News, which was once difficult and expensive to obtain, today surrounds us like the air we breathe. Much of it is literally ambient: displayed on computers, public billboards, trains, aircraft, and mobile phones. Where once news had to be sought out in expensive and scarce news sheets, today it is ubiquitous and very largely free at the point of consumption. Satisfying news hunger no longer involves a twice daily diet of a morning newspaper and evening TV news bulletin: news comes in snack-form, to be grazed, and at every level of quality; even to be programmed to order, to arrive, presorted, via your personal digital assistant. Where once journalism's reach was confined by the time it took to haul bundles of newsprint from one end of a country to the other, now it is global, instantaneous, and interactive.

But there are problems with this new culture of news. Because there is so much of it, we find it difficult to sort the good from the bad. The fact that it is mostly obtainable without direct payment may mean that we value it less. As a generation grows up unaccustomed to the idea that news costs money, the economics of resource-intensive journalism, like in-depth investigations, are undermined.

Forthcoming
Photography, Steve Edwards

Chapter 7
Are we all mad?

Introduction   **Dylan Evans**

The human mind faces many challenges in its quest for knowledge, but none greater than the challenge of understanding itself. For many centuries, people did not even know what the mind *was*, let alone how it worked. Most people assumed that the mind was a spiritual substance, quite unlike the material body it inhabited. The eventual recognition that the mind is, in fact, not a spiritual thing – that it is, in fact, not a 'thing' at all, but a process carried out by a purely material organ (the brain) – is probably the most important scientific discovery of all time. But this is just the beginning. We now face the daunting task of discovering *how the mind works*. Since the brain is the most complex object in the known universe, this task is not going to be easy (see *The Brain: A Very Short Introduction*).

It is still early days. Scientific psychology is barely more than 100 years old (see *Psychology: A Very Short Introduction*). Our current knowledge of the mind is probably as rudimentary as our knowledge of physics was in the 17th century, before Newton wrote the *Principia*. Psychology has yet to find its Newton.

Some have laid claim to that title. Sigmund Freud (1856–1939), for example, compared his theory of the unconscious to the revolutionary discoveries of Copernicus and Darwin (see *Freud: A Very Short Introduction*). Similar claims were made by one of Freud's early disciples, Carl Gustav Jung (1875–1961) (see *Jung:*

A Very Short Introduction). History has not borne out these claims, however; the ideas of both Freud and Jung have since been superseded by more accurate theories. Our current theories will themselves be superseded as we continue to make progress in discovering how the mind works.

The theory of evolution by natural selection will no doubt play a key role in future developments in psychology. Natural selection has shaped our minds just as it has shaped our bodies, so we should expect our minds to be good at enabling us to do things that help us survive and reproduce. Intelligence, a notoriously difficult concept to define, can perhaps be best understood as the ability to solve adaptive problems (see *Intelligence: A Very Short Introduction*). Emotions play a key role in this ability, and are increasingly seen not as an impediment to intelligent action, but as a vital component of intelligence (see *Emotion: A Very Short Introduction*).

Like all products of evolution, the mind has its fair share of design flaws. It can break down in a number of ways, and the history of our attempts to understand these disorders is a fascinating tale (see *Psychiatry: A Very Short Introduction*). The most severe disorder is schizophrenia, with its bizarre hallucinations and strange delusions (see *Schizophrenia: A Very Short Introduction*).

Perhaps the greatest challenge of all in understanding the mind will be to understand consciousness (see *Consciousness: A Very Short Introduction*). At the dawn of the 21st century, there is still no scientific consensus about what consciousness is. If 99% of what the mind does can be done without consciousness, why not do all of it unconsciously? And what is it that determines which thoughts, of the millions fizzing around our brains, should enter conscious awareness? And why do we have little islands of consciousness in the great ocean of unconsciousness that we call sleep?

If we understood what consciousness was, and how it worked, we might even be able to build a conscious machine. In fact, artificial intelligence is the ultimate test for all our psychological theories. Only when we can build robots with minds like ours will be able to say, with confidence, that we truly understand how our minds work.

www.dylan.org.uk

Psychology   **Gillian Butler and Freda McManus**

Psychology, as defined by William James, is about the mind or brain, but although psychologists do study the brain, they do not understand enough about its workings to be able to comprehend the part that it plays in the expression of our hopes, fears, and wishes, or in our behaviour during experiences as varied as giving birth or watching a football match. Indeed, it is rarely possible to study the brain directly. So, psychologists have discovered much more by studying our behaviour, and by using their observations to derive hypotheses about what is going on inside us.

Psychology is also about the ways in which organisms, usually people, use their mental abilities, or minds, to operate in the world around them. The ways in which they do this have changed over time as their environment has changed. Evolutionary theory suggests that if organisms do not adapt to a changing environment they will become extinct (hence the sayings 'adapt or die' and 'survival of the fittest'). The mind has been, and is still being, shaped by adaptive processes. This means that there are evolutionary reasons why our minds work the way they do – for instance, the reason we are better at detecting moving objects than stationary ones may be because this ability was useful in helping our ancestors to avoid predators. It is important for psychologists, as well as for those working in other scientific disciplines such as biology and physiology, to be aware of those reasons.

'very readable, stimulating, and well-written'

Anthony Clare

Intelligence   Ian J. Deary

The question of how to conceive of human mental capacities is a vexed one. Psychologists have argued about it for most of the 20th century, and the debate continues. The first person to describe the general factor in human intelligence was an English army officer turned psychologist, Charles Spearman, in a famous research paper in 1904. He examined schoolchildren's scores in different academic subjects. The scores were all positively correlated, and he put this down to a general mental ability. There followed decades of arguments among psychologists as to whether or not there was such a single entity.

Indications of intelligence

i)   There is a modest association between brain size and psychometric intelligence. People with bigger brains tend to have higher mental test scores. We do not know yet why this association occurs.

ii) People with higher intelligence, on average, appear to elicit faster, more complex, and differently shaped electrical responses when brain activity is recorded by an electroencephalogram (EEG) machine.

iii) There is a well-established, moderate association between the efficiency of the early stages of visual perception and intelligence test scores.

iv) People with higher intelligence test scores have, on average, shorter and less variable reaction times.

Are we all mad?

'*extremely readable ... Without dumbing down or patronising the reader, Ian Deary has done the general public a great service.*'

Journal of Nursing

Schizophrenia   **Chris Frith and Eve Johnstone**

What is schizophrenia?

Schizophrenia is the term applied to a severe form of mental disorder, which can be observed in all countries and cultures. At a rough estimate, about 1 person in 100 may experience this disorder at some time in their lives. This life-time risk of 1% is about the same as that for developing rheumatoid arthritis. Many of us will know of someone with this much more visible disorder. The experience of schizophrenia is extremely distressing both for the sufferer and for his or her family and friends. The monetary cost of schizophrenia is also severe. In terms of care and treatment, the annual cost of schizophrenia in the UK in the early 1990s was £397 million, while the indirect costs in terms of lost production were conservatively estimated at the same time to be £1.7 billion.

Drugs   **Leslie Iversen**

The 20th century saw a remarkable upsurge of research on drugs, with major advances in the treatment of bacterial and viral infections, heart disease, stomach ulcers, cancer, and mental illnesses. These, along with the introduction of the oral contraceptive, have altered all of our lives.

Recreational drugs

The total annual worldwide market for all medical drugs is approximately $250 billion, but the market for recreational drugs is probably at least ten times greater.

Alcohol: the pleasurable intoxicant actions of alcohol seem to be due in part to its ability to stimulate opiate mechanisms in the brain – the same ones that are stimulated more directly and more aggressively by heroin.

Nicotine: acts in the brain on receptors for the chemical messenger acetylcholine. The nerve tracts that release acetylcholine in the brain have among their functions the ability to act as an alerting or arousal system for the cerebral hemispheres – the thinking part of the brain.

Caffeine: one explanation for the stimulant effects of the drug is that by blocking the normal braking actions of adenosine the drug promotes more release of the chemicals acetylcholine and dopamine, both of which have stimulant effects on brain function.

Cannabis: the principal psychoactive ingredient in the plant is the complex chemical delta-9-tetrahydrocannabinol (THC) – there is a specific receptor protein in the brain that recognizes THC (a chemical found only in the cannabis plant).

Amphetamines: one of the first man-made recreational drugs, the military started the first non-medical use of the drug during the Second World War, to keep pilots and other military personnel awake and alert during long missions.

Heroin: in addition to the hazards inherent in the drug itself, users are likely to die from overdose because the street drug is of variable potency and quality, and at high doses the drug depresses respiration.

Cocaine: was incorporated into a number of freely available tonic 'coca-wines', and was an ingredient in the original Coca Cola®, until its dangers were recognized.

'illuminating'   TNT magazine

Emotion   **Dylan Evans**

Like language, colour, and music, drugs are an ancient form of emotional technology. Alcohol may have been invented as recently as 5,000 or 6,000 years ago, but there is archaeological evidence that humans began using other psychotropic drugs long before this.

Scientific interest in the emotions underwent something of a renaissance in the 1990s. For much of the 20th century, research in the emotions was confined to a few psychologists and even fewer anthropologists. At the dawn of the 21st century, however, things are rather different. Cognitive psychologists have abandoned their exclusive focus on reasoning, perception, and memory, and are rediscovering the importance of affective processes.

'a pop science classic'   Independent on Sunday

Freud   **Anthony Storr**

Everything

Sigmund Freud revolutionized the way in which we think about ourselves. From its beginnings as a theory of neurosis, Freud developed psychoanalysis into a general psychology which became widely accepted as the predominant mode of discussing personality and interpersonal relationships.

Freud and dreams

Freud affirmed that, with very few exceptions, dreams were disguised, hallucinatory fulfilments of repressed wishes, often dating from early childhood. This theory is clearly derived from, or comparable with, Freud's early statement about hysteria, in which he supposed that the trauma which provoked the current symptoms did so only because it awoke memories of traumata in childhood. He felt the interpretation of dreams provided a way into the unconscious activities of the mind.

'lucid, fair and astonishingly comprehensive'   Spectator

unreasonable therefore to suppose that such a machine must be endowed with miraculous properties. But while the world is full of mystery, science has no place for miracles and the 21st century's most challenging scientific problem is nothing short of explaining how the brain works in purely material terms.

Forthcoming
Child Development, Richard Griffin
Psychiatry, Tom Burns

Visit the
VERY SHORT
INTRODUCTIONS
Web site

www.oup.co.uk/vsi

➤ **Information** about all published titles

➤ News of **forthcoming books**

➤ **Extracts** from the books, including titles not yet published

➤ **Reviews** and views

➤ **Links** to other **web sites** and main OUP web page

➤ Information about **VSIs in translation**

➤ **Contact** the editors

➤ **Order** other **VSIs** on-line

CLASSICS
A Very Short Introduction
Mary Beard and John Henderson

This Very Short Introduction to Classics links a
haunting temple on a lonely mountainside to the glory
of ancient Greece and the grandeur of Rome, and to
Classics within modern culture – from Jefferson and
Byron to Asterix and Ben-Hur.

'The authors show us that Classics is a "modern" and
sexy subject. They succeed brilliantly in this regard ...
nobody could fail to be informed and entertained – and
the accent of the book is provocative and stimulating.'

John Godwin, *Times Literary Supplement*

'Statues and slavery, temples and tragedies, museum,
marbles, and mythology – this provocative guide to the
Classics demystifies its varied subject-matter while
seducing the reader with the obvious enthusiasm and
pleasure which mark its writing.'

Edith Hall

MUSIC
A Very Short Introduction
Nicholas Cook

This stimulating Very Short Introduction to music
invites us to really *think* about music and the values
and qualities we ascribe to it.

'A *tour de force*. Nicholas Cook is without doubt one of
the most probing and creative thinkers about music we
have today.'

Jim Samson, University of Bristol

'Nicholas Cook offers a perspective that is clearly influenced by recent writing in a host of disciplines related
to music. It may well prove a landmark in the appreci-
ation of the topic … In short, I can hardly imagine it being
done better.'

Roger Parker, University of Cambridge

www.oup.co.uk/vsi/music

PHILOSOPHY
A Very Short Introduction
Edward Craig

This lively and engaging book is the ideal introduction for anyone who has ever been puzzled by what philosophy is or what it is for.

Edward Craig argues that philosophy is not an activity from another planet: learning about it is just a matter of broadening and deepening what most of us do already. He shows that philosophy is no mere intellectual pastime: thinkers such as Plato, Buddhist writers, Descartes, Hobbes, Hume, Hegel, Darwin, Mill and de Beauvoir were responding to real needs and events – much of their work shapes our lives today, and many of their concerns are still ours.

'A vigorous and engaging introduction that speaks to the philosopher in everyone.'

John Cottingham, University of Reading

'addresses many of the central philosophical questions in an engaging and thought-provoking style . . . Edward Craig is already famous as the editor of the best long work on philosophy (the Routledge Encyclopedia); now he deserves to become even better known as the author of one of the best short ones.'

Nigel Warburton, The Open University

www.oup.co.uk/isbn/0-19-285421-6

LITERARY THEORY
A Very Short Introduction
Jonathan Culler

Literary Theory is a controversial subject. Said to have transformed the study of culture and society in the past two decades, it is accused of undermining respect for tradition and truth, encouraging suspicion about the political and psychological implications of cultural products instead of admiration for great literature. In this Very Short Introduction, Jonathan Culler explains 'theory', not by describing warring 'schools' but by sketching key 'moves' that theory has encouraged and speaking directly about the implications of cultural theory for thinking about literature, about the power of language, and about human identity. This lucid introduction will be useful for anyone who has wondered what all the fuss is about or who wants to think about literature today.

> 'It is impossible to imagine a clearer treatment of the subject, or one that is, within the given limits of length, more comprehensive. Culler has always been remarkable for his expository skills, and here he has found exactly the right method and tone for his purposes.'
>
> **Frank Kermode**

www.oup.co.uk/vsi/literarytheory

PSYCHOLOGY
A Very Short Introduction
Gillian Butler and Freda McManus

Psychology: A Very Short Introduction provides an up-to-date overview of the main areas of psychology, translating complex psychological matters, such as perception, into readable topics so as to make psychology accessible for newcomers to the subject. The authors use everyday examples as well as research findings to foster curiosity about how and why the mind works in the way it does, and why we behave in the ways we do. This book explains why knowing about psychology is important and relevant to the modern world.

'a very readable, stimulating, and well-written introduction to psychology which combines factual information with a welcome honesty about the current limits of knowledge. It brings alive the fascination and appeal of psychology, its significance and implications, and its inherent challenges.'

Anthony Clare

'This excellent text provides a succinct account of how modern psychologists approach the study of the mind and human behaviour. ... the best available introduction to the subject.'

Anthony Storr

www.oup.co.uk/vsi/psychology

ISLAM
A Very Short Introduction
Malise Ruthven

Islam features widely in the news, often in its most militant versions, but few people in the non-Muslim world really understand the nature of Islam.

Malise Ruthven's Very Short Introduction contains essential insights into issues such as why Islam has such major divisions between movements such as the Shi'ites, the Sunnis, and the Wahhabis, and the central importance of the Shar'ia (Islamic law) in Islamic life. It also offers fresh perspectives on contemporary questions: Why is the greatest 'Jihad' (holy war) now against the enimies of Islam, rather than the struggle against evil? Can women find fulfilment in Islamic societies? How must Islam adapt as it confronts the modern world?

> 'Malise Ruthven's book answers the urgent need for an introduction to Islam. ... He addresses major issues with clarity and directness, engages dispassionately with the disparate stereotypes and polemics on the subject, and guides the reader surely through urgent debates about fundamentalism.'
>
> **Michael Gilsenan, New York University**

www.oup.co.uk/vsi/islam

ARCHAEOLOGY
A Very Short Introduction
Paul Bahn

This entertaining Very Short Introduction reflects the enduring popularity of archaeology – a subject which appeals as a pastime, career, and academic discipline, encompasses the whole globe, and surveys 2.5 million years. From deserts to jungles, from deep caves to mountain tops, from pebble tools to satellite photographs, from excavation to abstract theory, archaeology interacts with nearly every other discipline in its attempts to reconstruct the past.

'very lively indeed and remarkably perceptive … a quite brilliant and level-headed look at the curious world of archaeology'
Barry Cunliffe, University of Oxford

'It is often said that well-written books are rare in archaeology, but this is a model of good writing for a general audience. The book is full of jokes, but its serious message – that archaeology can be a rich and fascinating subject – it gets across with more panache than any other book I know.'
Simon Denison, editor of *British Archaeology*

www.oup.co.uk/vsi/archaeology

HISTORY
A Very Short Introduction
John H. Arnold

History: A Very Short Introduction is a stimulating essay about how we understand the past. The book explores various questions provoked by our understanding of history, and examines how these questions have been answered in the past. Using examples of how historians work, the book shares the sense of excitement at discovering not only the past, but also ourselves.

'A stimulating and provocative introduction to one of collective humanity's most important quests – understanding the past and its relation to the present. A vivid mix of telling examples and clear cut analysis.'

David Lowenthal, University College London

'This is an extremely engaging book, lively, enthusiastic and highly readable, which presents some of the fundamental problems of historical writing in a lucid and accessible manner. As an invitation to the study of history it should be difficult to resist.'

Peter Burke, Emmanuel College, Cambridge

www.oup.co.uk/vsi/history

Expand your collection of
VERY SHORT INTRODUCTIONS

The brains of people with acquired blindness have developed perceptual capacities. Dreaming is the time in which people with acquired blindness see most clearly.

'engaging new book'   The Sunday Telegraph

Consciousness   **Susan Blackmore**

Defining consciousness

There is no generally agreed definition of consciousness, but the following gives some idea of what is meant by the word.

'What it's like to be ...': If there is something it is like to be an animal (or computer, or baby) then that thing is conscious. Otherwise it is not.

Subjectivity or **phenomenality**: Consciousness means subjective experience or phenomenal experience. This is the way things seem to me, as opposed to how they are objectively.

Qualia: The ineffable subjective qualities of experience, such as the redness of red or the indescribable smell of turpentine. Some philosophers claim they do not exist.

The hard problem: How do subjective experiences arise from objective brains?

The Brain   **Michael O'Shea**

Think for few moments about a very special machine, your brain – an organ of just 1.2 kg, containing one hundred billion nerve cells, none of which alone has any idea who or what you are. In fact the very idea that a cell can have an idea seems silly. A single cell after all is far too simple an entity. However, conscious awareness of one's self comes from just that: nerve cells communicating with one another by a hundred trillion interconnections. When you think about it this is a deeply puzzling fact of life. It may not be entirely

Jung   **Anthony Stevens**

However fortunate our upbringing may have been, few of us by middle age can hope to be any more than a 'good enough' version of the Self. One can, nevertheless, follow the Apollonian advice to 'know thyself', heed Pindar's dictum 'Become what thou art', and learn from Plato and Aristotle to discover one's 'true self' – to make explicit what implicitly one already is. In Jungian terms this means overcoming the divisions imposed by the parental and cultural milieu, to divest oneself of 'the false wrappings of the persona', and abandon one's ego-defences. It also involves avoiding projecting one's shadow on to others, but striving to know it and acknowledge it as part of one's inner life, and attempting to bring to conscious fulfilment the supreme intentions of the Self. Complete achievement of these objectives within the compass of one individual lifetime is never possible, of course, but that is not the point.

'The goal is important only as an idea,' wrote Jung; 'the essential thing is the *opus* which leads to the goal: *that* is the goal of a lifetime.'

> '*accessible, authoritative but, above all, very readable*'
> Clinical Psychology Forum

Dreaming   **J. Allan Hobson**

Do blind people see in their dreams?

People who are blind from birth have no visual imagery at any time, neither in waking nor in dreaming. Vision is not the only modality in visually impaired individuals; bodily sensations or the sense of position of the body in space is markedly enhanced, so these individuals do have other hallucinatory dream experiences.